IRAN

INTRODUCTION BY JAMES MORRIS

PHOTOGRAPHS BY ROGER WOOD

NOTES ON THE PLATES BY DENIS WRIGHT

with 141 photogravure plates, 10 colour plates and a map

I.A.D.A. LTD (MEBSO BOOKSHOP) TEHRAN

This edition specially prepared for I.A.D.A. Ltd (Mebso Bookshop) Tehran

TEXT © 1969 THAMES AND HUDSON LTD LONDON

PHOTOGRAPHS © 1969 ROGER WOOD

ALL RIGHTS RESERVED. NO PART OF THIS PUBLICATION MAY BE

REPRODUCED, STORED IN A RETRIEVAL SYSTEM, OR TRANSMITTED,

IN ANY FORM OR BY ANY MEANS, ELECTRONIC, MECHANICAL,

PHOTOCOPYING, RECORDING OR OTHERWISE, WITHOUT THE PRIOR

PERMISSION OF THE PUBLISHERS

TEXT FILMSET IN GREAT BRITAIN BY KEYSPOOLS LTD GOLBORNE AND

PRINTED IN GERMANY BY ENSSLIN AND LAIBLIN KG REUTLINGEN

COLOUR BLOCKS ENGRAVED IN SWITZERLAND BY HERM. DENZ AG BERNE AND

PRINTED IN GERMANY BY J FINK STUTTGART

PHOTOGRAVURE PLATES PRINTED IN FRANCE BY ETS BRAUN ET CIE MULHOUSE

BOUND IN GERMANY BY GROSSBUCHBINDEREI SIGLOCH KUNZELSAU

500 24067 1

CONTENTS

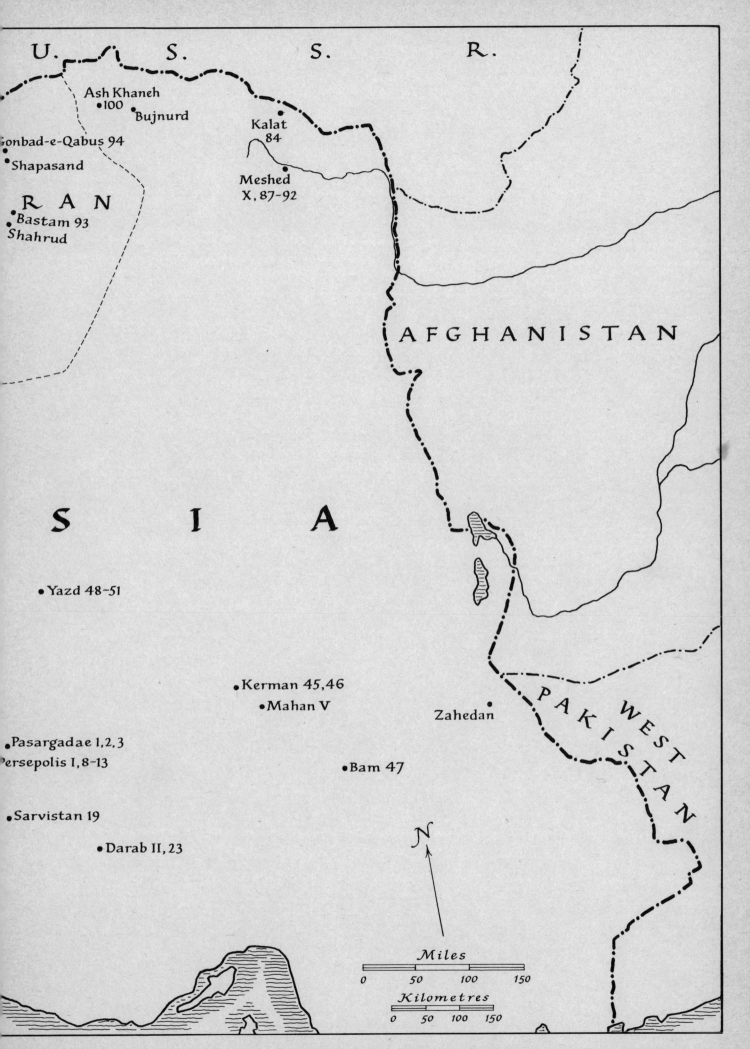

U. S. S. R.

Ash Khaneh
•100
Bujnurd

Kalat
84

Gonbad-e-Qabus 94
•Shapasand

Meshed
X, 87–92

RAN
•Bastam 93
Shahrud

AFGHANISTAN

S   I   A

•Yazd 48–51

•Kerman 45,46
•Mahan V

Zahedan•

WEST PAKISTAN

•Pasargadae 1,2,3
Persepolis I,8–13

•Bam 47

•Sarvistan 19

•Darab II,23

N

Miles

| 0 | 50 | 100 | 150 |

Kilometres

| 0 | 50 | 100 | 150 |

The numbers on the map refer to the Plates and corresponding Notes

THE MOST PERSIAN THING I know in Persia is the brick tower called Gonbad-e-Qabus, the Dome of Qabus, which was built in 1006 to house the corpse of Shams el Ma'ali Qabus, King of the Ziyarids.

Not long ago this marvellous object stood in lofty isolation among the Gorgan steppes, south-east of the Caspian Sea. Today it forms a totemic centre-piece for a boom town. The steppe has been reclaimed for wheat-growing. The little town of Gonbad blazes with new offices, apartments, cars and cafés, and has boulevards wide enough for a Parisian parade, and street lighting bright enough to dazzle Manhattan. On a hump in the middle stands the tower. At night the lights from the streets below illuminate the lower half of the building, and make it look like a flood-lit mill chimney: but the top part soars out of range of neon or headlight, deepens in mystery as it rises, and is silhouetted at the summit only against the ink-blue of the Persian night, studded ostentatiously with stars.

Whatever this structure is, it is not what we would call a dome, and it awakens no echoes in the western mind. Not many of us know who Shams el Ma'ali was, and not many more have ever heard of the Ziyarids. Architecturally the tower is a mystery. It is 167 feet high, and it tapers reluctantly, between buttresses, to a conical green roof. Nobody knows how it served the office of a mausoleum, though tradition says the king's body was suspended in a glass coffin high inside the tower. Russian scholars, supposing he was more probably buried *beneath* it, once sank a shaft through the foundations, but found only solid brick for 35 feet. In the roof there is a little window, facing east, and two inscriptions in Kufic script run right round the building. Once, a legend says, some sort of flashing object shone from the top, like a lighthouse in the steppe.

That is all. For the rest, the Dome of Qabus stands there tremendously blank, utterly unlike any other monument in the world. The town planners, offended perhaps by its enigmatic indifference, have laid out a garden on its mound, with ornamental steps and shrubberies: but the old prodigy disdains mere prettiness, and seems to be communicating with other worlds altogether, beyond the horizons of the ordinary.

In this it suggests an emblem of Persia. In 1935 the reforming autocrat Reza Shah Pahlevi decreed that his country should no longer be called Persia at all. Persia was the name, as he rightly said, of a particular region – Fars, which provided the first imperial dynasty, and gave its language to the nation, but which was after all only one among many provinces. In future, Reza Shah announced, his kingdom would be called Iran. This was a fashionable generic, from the same root as 'Aryan', which could embrace all the shifting and varied peoples of the Iranian plateau; it was welcomed fervently by nationalists, academically by scholars, willy-nilly by diplomatists and compilers of reference books.

Somehow, though, like that Dome of Qabus, 'Persia' rose above it all. It was a name that meant so much to the world: it was a figure of ancient splendours, poetry, turquoise domes in rose-gardens, turbaned sportsmen in the Maidan of Isfahan, Hentyan crises of Victorian imperialism, Omar Khayyam, the Silk Route, the host of Xerxes approaching the pass at Thermopylae, dromedaries and miniatures, wines of Shiraz, nightingales, Persian carpets, Persian markets, Persian cats (and Persian ticks, so the Oxford Dictionary warily suggests – 'argus persicus, found in houses in some parts of Persia'). Romantics and Englishmen clung to the word, and fourteen years later Reza Shah's son Mohammed Reza Shah Pahlevi, perhaps having a weakness for it himself, restored the old name to favour. Iran is still the official title of his country, and is used invariably for affairs of state, politics or economics: but Persia is back again as well, to express all the sensuous delights, echoes and memories of this most sensuous country.

The Persian allure is oblique, or allusive. This is not a country, like Spain or Britain, that stands theatrically distinct and complete. There is nothing insular about Persia. She has always been a bridge-country. She has frontiers with Arabs, Afghans, Turks, Pakistanis, Russians. She has ancient connections with Greeks, Romans, Chinese, Indians, Egyptians, Mongols, and tangled modern relationships with the British and the Americans. Persia was Alexander's ultimate enemy, and his most dazzling conquest: through the Persian caravan cities passed the Silk Route from China, a tenuous link between the civilizations of east and west. Persia is not easy terrain, but she offers the best-known and most practicable land route from Asia into Europe. Strategists of every age, Parthian to Pentagon, have recognized her importance.

Physically Persia is formidable. The shape of this country is a distorted square, as though it has been melted in a furnace, and allowed to set crooked. Down its western flank, from the Turkish frontier to the Gulf of Oman, run the Zagros mountains, so strong a barrier that some American strategists of the 1950s argued them to be the true boundary of the western world, beyond which all might be regarded as expendable. Across the top of Persia, at the southern end of the Caspian Sea, runs a narrower but still higher mountain range, the Elburz, which looms away eastward to the Afghan frontier, snowy all the year. Within these barricades lies the high Persian plateau, much of it desert and most of it more than 4,000 feet high. In the Caspian provinces north of the Elburz there are cornfields, tea-gardens, paddy-fields. At the southern end of the Zagros a blistered flat coastline straggles morosely towards the Indian Ocean. For the rest Persia consists of wind-scoured, sand-swept, sun-scorched upland, petering away from delectable orchard country to wilderness of infinite desolation.

It is essentially a desert place. Images of the desert dominate the Persian scene, and much of the Persian tang and vitality springs by reaction from its arid presence. The sandstorms which come billowing in waves of reds and greys out of the mountain gulleys abrade the plateau of flab or superfluity, and as they eddy away small clear visions of desert life are left hanging like mirages in the memory: a flock of goats and sheep jostling each other through a golden halo of dust, with two superior donkeys like prefects in the middle; heroic nomad women of the south, tousle-haired and blackened by the sun, the hems of their blinding flounced petticoats sweeping grandly in the sand; neat little grey and white pigeons twitching their flight across the Persian wastes; camel-trains, still lurching to market with tinkling bells and old men flopped like bundles of old clothes on high swaying humps; or a little goatherd with his animals, all heads down against the rasping wind, his trousers, jacket, turban all aflap, marching gravely across an apparently illimitable emptiness towards some unimaginable destination.

Noblest of all these desert evocations is a migration of the southern tribes, the Bakhtiari or Qashqai of the Zagros mountains. These redoubtable peoples spend their winters in the hot lowlands, their summers in high mountain valleys where their flocks can graze: and twice a year they can be seen on the move from one to the other – a whole community on the march, in a style and on a scale that suggests some epic migration of antiquity, a sweep of gypsies or a legendary trek of American Indians. Sheep and goats go first in their meandering flocks, chivvied by boys in a desultory nibbling progress, and behind them labour the camels and donkeys, lashed high with mounds of baggage and crowned by women and children. All about swagger the tribesmen, predatory-looking men of confused clothing, and on the dry air there rides a concert of shouts, bleats and bells, the woolly rustle of sheep, the jangling of copper pans, the modest clip-clop of donkey-hoofs. Slowly, slowly they move across the landscape, all these sights and noises made miniature by the size of the setting: twice a year for ever, obeying what seems to be less an economic impulse than an ineradicable instinct.

The Persian deserts are often pock-marked with the round air-holes of *qanats*, underground channels which connect the water-table with farms and villages. They are anything up to thirty miles long, may entail the digging of a shaft several hundred feet deep, have been a unique Persian speciality for many centuries, and form a prodigiously complex system of water distribution. The long tramping lines of their air-holes are inescapable: but these strange evidences of human vigour, silently crossing the landscapes in their countless thousands, do nothing to tame the Persian experience, but only dramatize its scale and strangeness.

Rich mixtures have made Persia what she is: cultural strains from all quarters, elixirs of snow-peak and desert and rainbelt, criss-cross traffic of trade and strategy. Through, around and over her the great world passes. Like a farmhouse left defiant between motorways, she has absorbed many an alien noise and odour, and accustomed herself to startling changes of pace, while insisting constantly and sometimes testily on her rights. Persia has been repeatedly invaded during her history, and her rulers have often been foreigners, yet the Persians have remained remarkably themselves. Scores of

I PERSEPOLIS, DOORWAY OF THE PALACE OF XERXES

The bas-relief shows Xerxes attended by two servants, one of them carrying a towel and fly whisk, the other a ceremonial umbrella over the King's head. There are several such doorways standing in the *Hadish*, or Palace of Xerxes, and two similar ones, depicting Darius, in the nearby *Tripylon*, or Central Palace. In Achaemenian and Sassanian Persia the umbrella was, as it still is in parts of Africa today, a symbol of royalty or authority.

II DARAB, SASSANIAN BAS-RELIEF

The Sassanians carved majestic sculptures out of the living rock, mostly in their native province of Fars, designed to exalt their kings and perpetuate their fame. Their three main rock sites are at Naqsh-e-Rustam (Plates 5, 6), Shapur, 76 miles west of Shiraz, and Taq-e-Bustan (Plate 15), at all of which there are a series of rock carvings of royal triumphs.

At Darab, on a sandstone ridge lying between the modern town and the circular Parthian walls of ancient Darabgerd, there is this large Sassanian rock sculpture carefully sited in a rock-cut niche above a pool of clear water. It shows the Roman Emperors, Philip the Arab and Valerian (the latter having been decisively defeated and made prisoner by Shapur I at Edessa in AD 260), submitting to the Sassanian King. Behind the mounted Shapur are rows of Persian nobles and, opposite them, behind the two Roman Emperors, rows of Roman prisoners.

Three of the bas-reliefs at Shapur and one at Naqsh-e-Rustam (Plate 5) similarly record Shapur's victory over Valerian. (See also Plate 23.)

racial and religious minorities enrich Persian society, Jews and Zoroastrians and Assyrians and Armenians, Turkomens and Arabs and tribal strains from the Baluchi to the Kurdish, yet the people of the central plateau are recognizable anywhere. They are a dark, slight, hook-nosed, handsome lot. They have been given a dingy look by their adoption of western clothes, generally of drab textile and obsolete cut, but they still have Assyrian, bas-relief profiles, and their black eyes glint with an evasive humour, as though they wish to make you laugh, but have no intention of explaining the joke.

Foreigners frequently find something inexplicable about the Persians. They are a gifted, civilized and exceptionally charming people, but hard to catch. Their processes of thought are not apparent to western minds. Old Persia Hands used to say that if you asked a Persian which was his left ear, he would put his right hand behind his head and point it out from behind. Robert Byron, that irascible English traveller of the 1930s, made it plain in 230 pages of a clever and very funny book that he never really got to grips with Persian intentions, and intelligent Persian-speaking foreigners today often admit to an intellectual block: *'We don't know how well we know them'*. Miles and miles from anywhere in the Persian desert one day I saw two respectably dressed middle-aged men riding bicycles with bright panniers across the horribly corrugated surface of the sand. 'What on earth are they doing?' I asked my Persian companion. 'They are cyclists,' he replied.

Such erratic and disarming finality is one of the strengths of Persia – the strength of a *non sequitur*, which is unanswerable because of the blank in the middle. A lack of apparent logic, or rather logic well camouflaged, has helped Persia to retain her deeper dignity through many vicissitudes and humiliations. If I illustrate the trait with a comic

III Isfahan, Royal Mosque (Masjid-e-Shah)

Shah Abbas I (1586–1628), the greatest of the Safavid kings, made Isfahan his capital in 1598. With the help of architects and artisans from Europe, India and China he converted it into one of the world's most splendid cities. Luckily, many of his buildings still stand.

The Royal Mosque, begun about 1611 and finished in 1640, is the largest and most spectacular of his buildings. Arthur Upham Pope considers it 'among the world's greatest buildings'. Its scale is tremendous and the brilliance of its predominantly blue faience tiling almost overwhelming. Seen from the air the recessed and tiled entrance portal, flanked by two 110-ft. minarets, breaks into the two-storeyed façade of Shah Abbas's spacious Royal Maidan, or Square, seven times the size of the Piazza San Marco in Venice. The portal faces north in conformity with the alignment of the Maidan but, in order to set the axis of the mosque in the direction of Mecca, a skilfully contrived half-right turn is effected before entering the great central courtyard. (See also Plate 25.)

anecdote, it is not because the trait itself is comic, but because Persian characteristics are often served up soufflé style—their flavour fluffed about in humour, but none the less strong and subtle beneath. It is said of the great Reza Shah that he was once making an inspection tour down his new Trans-Iranian railway when a preceding loco-motive was derailed and capsized beside the track. The railway workers did not want His Imperial Majesty to see this evidence of their ineptitude. Desperately they worked to put the engine on the track again, or at least on its wheels, as the royal train sped down the line towards them. But they failed to move it an inch, and only just in time hit upon a spaciously Persian solution. They buried it.

Persia's ambiance is pungent and defensive – as distinctive a national flavour, perhaps, as any on earth – and the foreigner is easily absorbed by it. In the vaults of the Central Bank of Persia, in Tehran, are kept the Crown Jewels, an astonishing collection of gems and objets d'art which provide backing for the national currency. They have been assembled over several royal generations, and are rich in spoils of war, begemmed weapons, enormously expensive baubles and gifts from other kingly dynasties. Kept in a huge underground strongroom seething with plain-clothes men, the collection has become a great tourist attraction.

I was down there one day on a crowded weekday morning, among the blue-rinsed coiffures and jangling charm-bracelets of my fellow-marvellers, when I came across an agreeable case of brooches and little jewelled watches – more to my scale, I thought, than the colossal diamonds and tiered crowns that set the general tone of the exhibition. I stooped to examine these ornaments more closely, and as I did so the treasure-house suddenly reverberated with the ear-splitting blast of an alarm hooter. Everyone froze. Not a word was spoken. Not a pixie-charm tinkled. We waited aghast for the sound of splintered glass, gun-shots, hand-cuffs or explosions. The hooter went on hooting. For a moment nothing else happened: then a smart young woman in green walked with composure across the room. She avoided the case containing the Gika of Nadir Shah, with its diamond ornaments of bayonets and gun-barrels around a monumental emerald. She ignored the sceptre presented to Reza Shah by the people of Azerbaijan, with its gold lions rampant around a jewelled globe. She took no notice of the Sea of Light, sibling to the Koh-i-Noor, inherited from the first Mogul Emperor of India by way of the treasury of the Qajar tribe. Instead she walked calmly, with a loud clicking of her heels, directly across the vault to me.

'May I please ask you', she said with an amiable smile, 'to remove your elbow from that metal bar around the jewel-case?' I moved my arm. The hooter stopped. She thanked me. I kicked the last sand over the buried railway-engine, and the glory of Persia proceeded.

*

Darius, the greatest emperor of the original Persian empire, died in 485 BC, having extended the Achaemenian dynasty from Macedonia to the Indus. He had allied himself with the great winged god Ormuzd, without whose sanction nothing lasting could be achieved, and he was the master of Egypt, Libya, Turkey, Thrace and territories far beyond the Oxus. He was succeeded by Xerxes, whose fleets were routed by the Greeks at Salamis, and finally humiliated a century after his death by Alexander the Great, who put an end to the dynasty and ended Persia's golden age.

Darius, his son Xerxes, his grandson Artaxerxes and his great-grandson Darius II were all buried in rock tombs in a cliff called Naqsh-e-Rustam, near Persepolis – tombs cut so inaccessibly in the rock that Darius's own parents, so legend says, slipped and were killed when visiting his sarcophagus. There is a puzzling stone cube of a building opposite the cliff, and Sassanian kings later caused heroic reliefs to be carved among the tombs. It is, however, the presence of the dead Achaemenians that gives the site its majesty: a dry dead majesty, very old and long ago, that has lost all emanations of life or love, and now has only an intellectual magnetism.

I went to the tombs one night when the greatest of full moons, bigger and richer and more golden than Europe ever saw, was rising like some nobly-fulfilled dowager behind the Qashqai hills. Naqsh-e-Rustam was deserted. The attendant had packed away his ticket book and locked up his ugly wooden hut. The last of the little falcons that haunt the cliff had flitted into its crevice for the night. Only the headlights of the trucks flashed from the Shiraz road, and a couple of distant dogs barked at each other irritably in the darkness. The moonlight crept slowly up the cliff, over huge sculpted kings in their imperial poses, until it shone on the tombs themselves, flattening them against the cliff, so that their entrances were startlingly black with shadow, but their carved façades had lost all depth and detail, as though white gauze had been thrown over them.

I never knew a deader place that Naqsh-e-Rustam that night. It was as though those tremendous kings, whose names are written so large in the history of the world, had been no more than stone images in the first place. It was their power that created the first of the world empires; their ambition which summoned, if only by response, all the splendours of Marathon, Salamis and Thermopylae, whose telling can stir men even now. Yet they have left no vibrations in the air of Persia. I could conceive no ghosts that evening. I shouted their lordly names, but there was scarcely an echo. The place was numb.

The power of ancient Persia, though its monuments are very grand, is somehow seldom vivid. There is something lifeless to the genius of the Achaemenians. They were clearly great soldiers and fine administrators. Splendid communications bound their empire together, power was skilfully dispersed between the centre and the provinces, and the whole structure was maintained without resort to slavery. Yet as the tombs seem to possess no power of evocation, so the great Achaemenian capital of Persepolis arouses no affection nor even exactly admiration: only awe. It is difficult to imagine living people actually making use of Persepolis, and indeed it was apparently designed to be inhuman. Darius built it in isolation, removed from any city and aloof from the lives of ordinary folk. He built it upon a vast artificial platform, to plans which were obviously meant to be overbearing rather than pleasing – dark pillared audience chambers, enormous ceremonial staircases. Squat lions with double heads formed the capitals of pillars, and armies of sculpted images marched in disciplined bas-relief up panoramic staircases.

And these stone images of Persepolis provide a fitting bodyguard still to their vanished commanders. They have been wonderfully preserved (some of them having been buried under rubble for a couple of thousand years) and the relief is often as sharp as new. Strangers often take them to be reproductions. But far from making them more sprightly, this perfection only adds to their lifelessness. They are like newly-cast automatons moving in involuntary procession up those steps – all the same height, all in stiff step, all apparently the same age, all exactly graded, Medes and Persians, Elamites and Parthians, Scythians and Cappadocians, Afghans and Cilicians, Indians and Arabs, Ethiopians and Thracians – carrying golden ornaments, bows, lengths of cloth, pottery, daggers – leading horses, camels, lions, a giraffe, a wild ass – all with the same faces, all in the same attitudes, as though Darius and Xerxes had commissioned them all to be made to a standard mould, the originals no less than the images.

Alexander the Great may or may not have set fire to Persepolis, but he certainly put paid to its frigid glories, and destroyed its empire. The Persian dynasties which followed, alien or indigenous, never achieved such power again. The Greek Seleucids came and went. The Parthians stormed in from the north-west, held off Romans in the west and Scythians in the north, and gave the Persians a dashing sort of government for four centuries. The Sassanians, a dynasty from central Persia, drove out these aliens, and for 400 years provided a flamboyant series of monarchs: conquerors, lovers of horses and women, builders of big ugly palaces and patrons of epic bas-reliefs, proclaiming their own glories larger than life on rock-slabs all over Persia.

Confused with all these kings in the Persian memory, too, are the heroes of an immense body of myth – people half legendary, half historical, fable blended with fact. In the Persian sagas the Sassanian kings are apotheosized to stand beside the Sishrava of Indian folklore, the Laila of Arab romance, Alexander himself and a host of other misty warriors, sages and lovers. This demi-world of romance is much to the Persian taste, and the myth has become as real as the history. The Rustam of Naqsh-e-Rustam, where those emperors are buried, is the same tragic hero whose legend inspired Matthew Arnold, Her Majesty's Inspector of Schools. The Persian name for Persepolis is Takht-e-Jamshid – the throne of Jamshid, a monarch of less substantial splendour than Darius (*They say the Lion and the Lizard keep | The Courts where Jamshyd gloried and drank deep*).

Yet through these veils of legend and later history, through all the turmoil of wars and revolutions and dynastic rivalries, the flat images of the Achaemenians can be seen in clear silhouette, mighty emperors all in a row. They remain, if hardly the most lively, still the most forceful of the Persian rulers. Alexander, we are told, was much moved by the pathos of the conquered dynasty, so great a fact in the world of their heyday that the emperor of Persia was known to the west simply as Basileus – The King. The first great sovereign of the dynasty, the true founder of the Persian empire and so the father of Persia herself, was Cyrus the Great, who died in 530 BC. He seems to have been a good king, and he built himself a palace in a pleasant valley in Fars, at Pasargadae. There his tomb remains. It is a far gentler memorial than the tombs of his terrific successors – a square stone structure alone in pastureland, bleached by the sun and surrounded in later centuries by the graves of Muslims, who believed it to contain the corpse of Solomon's mother. It is a thing of kindly numen.

On this building, so Plutarch says, Cyrus had his own inscription carved: 'Grudge me not this little earth that covereth my body'. The young Alexander, arriving at Pasargadae in the course of conquest, was so affected by this inscription, and so angered to find the monument neglected by its guardians, that he ordered it to be restored and conserved for ever, and punished the keepers of the tomb for their infidelity.

In steamy gymnasiums of Tehran, or glimpsed through basement windows in fusty provincial bazaars, the members of the Houses of Strength perform their rituals. Here is something strange and striking. Dressed only in bright knee-length trousers, a dozen large sweating men do peculiar exercises in a pit, to the beat of a drum and the chanting of epic verse. They leap. They spin. They juggle unliftable clubs. They do push-ups on the floor, and gyrate with shields and iron bows. They throw themselves grunting upon one another in wrestling contests. And when the drumbeat ends, the poetry subsides, and the last wrestlers disentangle themselves exhausted from the clinch, they resume their sober brown suits and unobtrusive ties, pick up their briefcases or their workboxes, and step outside into the ordinary world as though they have merely been having a haircut.

The *Zurkhaneh* is a venerable Persian institution, so deep-rooted still that every day Tehran Radio broadcasts the drumbeats and the poems, to bring its mystique into the home. It smacks of secret societies and conspiracy, and with its militaristic trappings could be the nucleus of a resistance movement. This is probably what it originally was. It is a reminder that the Persia we know today, the Persia that has so enslaved the imagination of foreigners for five centuries and more, is essentially an innovation. There are older things about than the mosques and the carpets – not simply dead old things, like the tombs and the bas-reliefs of Persepolis, but old ways of thought, instincts, intuitions that are still alive.

It is the presence of this subculture, like an offbeat extra instrument to the orchestra of Islam, that gives the Persian civilization its unique fascination. Islam colonized Persia in the seventh century, and nearly everything we think of as most beautifully Persian springs from the faith in one way or another – the carpets, the pottery, the miniatures, the gardens, the architecture. Yet the Persians have never been absolutely reconciled to the *foreignness* of Islam, the fact that they were apostolized by force of arms: the fanatic zeal of the *Zurkhaneh*, though about as militant nowadays as a sauna bath or Olde Tyme Dancing, is a reminder of the fertile conflict between the old imperial pride of the Persians and their duty to Islam.

Persia is not a conformist member of the Islamic community of states. She remembers that the Arabs were her conquerors, and she lays claim to islands in the Persian Gulf which she maintains to have been hers before Islam was born. The Persians have been schismatic Muslims almost from the start, perhaps because they wished to give their beliefs a nationalist cast. The branch of Islam called Shi'ism, which recognizes its own successors to Mohammed, is a heresy among most Muslims, but is the official religion of Persia. The mystic movement called Sufism is powerful in this country, and it was a Shirazi, Mirza Ali Mohammed, who founded in 1844 the neo-Islamic religion called Baha'i, now a flourishing California cult. If one stands on the outskirts of Qazvin, beneath the southern slopes of the Elburz mountains, and looks northwards into the grim foothills of the range, ridge after tawny ridge, somewhere up there one may imagine the fortress-rock of Alamut. There the most fearful of all Islamic sects festered in the eleventh century – the Assassins, the Hashish Addicts, who lived there in fuddled and ferocious ecstasy under the command of their Grand Master, sometimes emerging down those dark valleys to murder a wazir or terrify a Sultan.

Cross-currents, undertows, complicate the flows of Persian Islam. The Persians were the most highly civilized of the nations overrun by the Arabs, and though they perforce adopted the Islamic culture themselves, they gave it exquisite refinements of their own. It was a culture born in the desert, and it throve on the contrasts between arid and arable, Earth and Paradise, that are so much a part of Persia's flavour. Half-a-dozen major Islamic dynasties have ruled Persia since the seventh century – Seljuks, Mongols, Timurids, Safavids, Qajars, Pahlevis. Some have been foreign, some native, and they have been interspersed by many periods of chaos, and characterized by rulers as frightful as Genghis Khan, as gorgeous as Tamerlane, as creative as Abbas the Great.

The dark and brutal periods interrupt the history of Islamic Persia like missing volumes in an encyclopedia, but the legacy as a whole is one of fastidious dignity. Wherever you go beautiful buildings of Islam greet you: grand crumbled mausoleums in insignificant hamlets, country mosques of startling brilliance, great brick domes in whose cool recesses the pigeons murmurously meditate, immense temples like the Shi'a shrine at Meshed or enchanting little tombs of holy men, conical-roofed like small blue pagodas in the damp Caspian country. When Persian patriots quote Hafez to us, as we walk in the gardens of their delight, it is an inexpressibly refined Muslim voice that we hear – a fatalistic voice, but not despondent, for if it expresses the transience of worldly glory, it also celebrates the joy of the passing moment:

> Sweet maid, if thou wouldst charm my sight,
> And bid these arms thy neck infold;
> That rosy cheek, that lily hand
> Would give thy poet more delight
> Than all Bokhara's vaunted gold,
> Than all the gems of Samarkand.

Since the Muslim conquest Persian art, once so warlike, has been above all precise, delicate, elegant: like the frail voice of a muezzin sailing the evening, or Arabic script on a parchment.

How the forms of the religion came to infuse every aspect of Persian life can best be seen at Isfahan, the city made famous by Abbas Shah the Safavid in the seventeenth century. Abbas made it his capital, and imported companies of craftsmen, artists, architects, gardeners and artisans to make it the most prosperous and beautiful city in Asia. It is hardly that now, for much of the original plan has since been spoiled, but its grand centre-piece remains – the Maidan-e-Shah, one of the largest piazzas on earth, seven times the size of the Piazza San Marco, and arguably (though not by me) more noble. On the west side of this square stands the Ali Qapu, a pleasure palace which Robert Byron likened to a boot-box, but which reminds me more of a race-track grandstand. From its pillared upstairs verandah, often a scene of opulent festivity but now more like a disused pier pavilion, we may still look over the Maidan like courtiers or envoys, and see how Islam inspired the Shah's town-planners.

At the northern end of the square a series of tunnels or caves appears to emerge out of the surrounding buildings into the sunlight. It is the Imperial Bazaar of Isfahan, once the greatest marketplace in Persia, and still hard at work. Scores of cars and taxis are lined up outside it, crowds swarm noisily in and out, buses of tourists come and go, through the clamour we may hear the clanging of metal-smiths or the shouts of itinerant sherbet-sellers. That faint haze we see about the entrance is as old as Isfahan, and is compounded of ancient dust-particles, emanations of spice, the solidified echoes of accumulated hagglings and generations of animal warmth.

The centre of the square, a quarter of a mile long, has lately been given over to orna-mental pools and gardens, illustrating Progress, and a few citizens are sitting in dispirited postures on its benches, or maundering along its finicky paths. Abbas laid it out, though, as a polo ground and tournament field, and at each end you may still see its squat stone polo posts. Marvellously dashing things went on down there – tilting contests, archery on horseback, fights between gladiators, between rams, between lions and bulls. Some, times the whole square was illuminated with 50,000 little lamps, and at nighttime in Isfahan, so the seventeenth-century traveller John Fryer tells us, all the grandees aired themselves, 'prancing about with their numerous trains, striving to outvie each other in Pomp and Generosity'.

But finally, as we raise our eyes above these scenes of authority, commerce and plain pleasure, we see the great square sanctioned and unified by religion. The mosques of the Arabs look down severely upon abstinence. The mosques of the Persians look down benignly upon the full variety of human life. Opposite us is the *café au lait* dome of Sheikh Lutfullah, a compact little masterpiece – no courtyard, no great gateway, only this lovely tiled dome over a single chamber, hidden away behind the arcade. And behind the goal posts at the southern end of the Maidan, at an angle to face Mecca, is the big multi-coloured tumble of the Royal Mosque, rising in gay but reverent tiers to the climax of its blue dome.

So a whole society is captured down there, at once disciplined and ennobled by the power of the faith, and all the ambiguities of Persian Islam are gloriously resolved. One inescapable element of Muslim architecture in Persia, however, is best experienced on the other side of Isfahan, away from this imperial plaza, this showpiece of kings. For that particular pleasure of *learned fun* which is so much a part of the Persian mystique, let us sit down beside the bridge called Pul-e-Khwaju, over the Zaindeh river about a mile from the square. It is not really a kingly sort of bridge, nor warlike, nor even tremendously

IV Isfahan, Theological College of the Mother of the Shah (Madresseh-e-Mader-e-Shah). Main Court

Peaceful as an Oxford quadrangle, the Madresseh's courtyard, here seen from the octagonal entrance vestibule, is entered by a stalactite-vaulted archway from the Chahar Bagh, Isfahan's busy principal thoroughfare. The doors are of wood covered with chased silver plates, part gilded. The stone basin seen in the foreground is cut from a single block of stone.

The Madresseh was built in the early 18th century according to the tradi-tional Persian mosque design of a vaulted *ivan*, or porch, centred in each of the four sides of a rectangular courtyard. The north *ivan* leads to a domed sanctuary chamber; two *ivans* served as lecture halls and the fourth as the entrance portal. The courtyard's façade consists of two storeys of arched alcoves with what were once students' rooms behind. The walls of the courtyard are decorated with polychrome tilework. (See also Plate 24.)

monumental; but it combines a rich functionalism with a sense of fizz—like the best Victorian architecture in England, and springing from the same combination of technical, social and spiritual certainty.

We sit on the sun-soaked golden stones, let us say, early on an exuberant morning, and wait for the life of the place to warm us. The bridge has many purposes. It takes a road across the river, of course, on a double tier of twenty-three arches: but it also sprouts gay polygonal pleasure-pavilions, and there is a weir beneath it. Its inside is hollow, a long vaulted arcade that smells of water and is dappled with the river's reflections. Flat weedy banks protrude into the stream about it, and above stand mauve mountains and a sky that is perceptibly hazed with sand.

Life stirs. A mullah comes striding vigorously over the weir, his cloak streaming: he looks at us fiercely over his beard, and disappears like an avenger up the opposite bank, towards the quarter of the Armenians, who make wine, and have a cathedral, and are in several other ways thorough-going infidels. Small boys appear next, to splash about in the shallow water, and leap ostentatiously across the deep sluices. Now a talkative party of women are hitching up their draperies and washing their carpets in the sluice-stream – partly to clean them, partly to make them look older for the tourist trade. On a mud-bank in mid-river two dogs are pointlessly chasing each other round and round, tongues lolling. At the corner of the bridge a man is setting up a lettuce stall, and a youth with a camera around his neck is lying in wait for susceptible visitors.

Cars are arriving now, to line themselves up on the pavement beside the bridge: blue rinses and bangles step out of some, harangued by indefatigable elderly guides, while out

V Mahan, shrine of Shah Nematullah Vali

Sayyed Nur-ud-din, better known by his religious title of Shah Nematullah Vali, was a mystic and poet who, after wanderings in Central Asia, settled in 1406 at Mahan, a small oasis surrounded by desert and bare mountains, 23 miles south-east of Kerman. He died there in 1431 after founding a Dervish Order which still has many devotees who annually make the pilgrimage to the shrine which was built over his grave in 1437.

Shah Nematullah's tomb lies beneath this large turquoise-blue dome dating from the reign of Shah Abbas I, who enlarged and embellished the shrine in 1601. There is no more lovely group of buildings than this in Persia. Four open courts, two on the east and two on the west side, lead to the shrine: with their flower-beds, tall pines, cypresses and shaded pools set against the turquoise dome and minarets, they create an air of peace and contentment in striking contrast to the asperities of the desert outside. Robert Byron scarcely exaggerated when he wrote that travellers arriving at Mahan thought they were in paradise.

of others emerge more carpet-washers, hauling big bundles tied up with string, and talking loudly as they trail down the bank to the sluices. Soon there must be forty or fifty people around the bridge, on the weir, under the arches, up and down the banks: we can catch glimpses of the traffic passing above us too, and once a woman all in black glides along the sidewalk up there, and we can watch her progress across the entire bridge, in snatches between each arch, like a ghost in a very old cinematograph performance. Now the whole place bustles with a festive diligence. Everyone is busy, if only in jumping over sluice-channels. The lettuce business seems to be brisk, carpets are ageing by half-centuries before our eyes, two American ladies smile heavily at the cameraman while their guide hovers out of frame with the familiar diffidence of one who expects his proper rake-off. There is a bleating of goats, a rush of water through the sluices, an occasional yap from the dogs on the mudbank.

In the shadowy underneath of the bridge a student sits, dangling his feet over a sluice, reading a book. His face is dark and meditative, and his air of poetic concentration is all one asks of a Persian student – in a country where the lyric poets of long ago, Hafez or Sa'di or Rumi, are still familiar and beloved among people of all ranks. But he has caught sight of us, in a dreamy sort of way, and as he buttons his jacket, gathers his notebooks and moves sidelong in our direction, we may recognize one of the more endearing hazards of Persian travel, the Student of English. We are too late to escape. 'Sir!' he cries, 'Madam!', fluttering his notebooks and bearing down on us. 'Allow me please to ask one question, before you leave the bridge: is it permissible or not, in the English language, to pursue a gerund with a participle? Would you be kind enough to comment upon my pronunciation in the following passage, Exercise 12? Sit down, sir, sit down, madam! Be comfortable!'

Out of Islam, too, the desert creed, came the preoccupation with oasis delights that has become so characteristic of Persia. The Arabs created their earthly paradises chiefly in the mind, imagining the gardens of Damascus to be far lovelier than they were, and clothing in hyperbole many a drab water-hole or date-grove. The Persians, seizing upon the fancy, turned it into fact. They made the desert a foil to their art, and used it as a painter uses a frame. The wall, a structural necessity both of desert life and of Islamic marriage, became in Persian hands an aesthetic device. The Persians became masters of the enclave, the secret garden, the courtyard, the arcade, the miniature, and all techniques by which the gross world outside could be contrasted with delicate privacies within. Seclusion is a high Persian virtue, and precision, the fastidious reduction from the scale of a wilderness to the scale of a flower, is half the Persian charm. Sir John Chardin, a seventeenth-century watchmaker who spent some years in Persia, unintentionally sums it up in a piece of technical information about Persian viniculture. So pure is the air of Persia, he says, that it is not necessary to cork a wine-bottle there: you need only place a rose or a carnation in the neck of the bottle, and all will be preserved.

No other desert people, I think, has tried to counter the immensity of a landscape not only with greenness, but also with smallness. The effect can be as refreshing as a little white-and-gold Colonial church perky among skyscrapers. There is a dirt road which crosses the hills called Kuh-i-Gazah, in central Persia, and drops down to the edge of the great desert on the eastern side, north of Kashan. I took it one spring day more or less at random, without a map, only knowing that it was sure to take me eastward. It was not a very encouraging route. The hills are bare and grey there, the road is very bumpy, there was scarcely a sign of human life, and I resigned myself to one of those semi-automatic phases of travel in which one switches off the sensibilities, in order to conserve them. Presently, however, passing through a narrow defile and turning a corner, I discovered one of Chardin's bottleneck carnations. Alone in a declivity in the hills, which now momentarily opened to reveal a ring of snow-summits beyond, there stood as lovely a human settlement, it seemed to me, as ever a traveller saw.

Fruit gardens were splashed all over the little plain, swathes of pink and white, framed with mud walls and supervised by pigeon-towers. A stream trickled beside the track. The village was a cluster of balconies, gardens, mud walls and poplars, with a blue-coned shrine in an orchard, a derelict fort, the four-square compound of a caravanserai, and presiding over it all on the slope of the hills, the very dream of a mosque—a dome of turquoise and yellow, four turquoise and yellow minarets, and seven small polychromatic spikes poised in attendance all about. Nothing moved in the village, as I sat in the car contemplating this celestial scene. The people, I suppose, were all at work, or food, or prayer, or very likely love. A scented hush lay over the scene, and everything shone.

Just over the ridge lay the desert, and presently I drove on, and entered the brown hangdog streets of Kashan, where a garage man told me that the village was probably Joshagan, once famous for its carpets. But I did not care what its name was. It really had seemed, as the Persian planners would have wished it, a passing suggestion of Paradise: and though everything about it seemed in retrospect small and meticulous, yet the whole was most dignified. The Persians do not equate smallness with meanness: perhaps in a largely arid country three times the area of France, they know how niggling size can be.

The celebrated gardens of Persia are no less a response to the desert. There is a world of difference between the Persian garden and the great gardens created by the Moors in Spain, at the other end of Islam. The Persians made nothing like the Generalife, that lush prodigy of foliage and fountains above Granada. In Persia the materials were less lavish, the water was more valuable, and Paradise was seen in terms that were almost Zen-like in their restraint. It was a Persian poet whose lines were carved upon a palace wall: 'If there be a Paradise on earth, it is here, it is here, it is here': but they were carved upon the wall of a palace majestic chiefly in its chaste austerity, beneath a blazing sky on a dust hillock in Delhi.

The foreigner is generally disappointed in the gardens of Persia. The legendary bowers of Shiraz do not, to an English eye, compare for charm with an Oxford garden, for splendour with the terraced gardens of Ceylon or the Caribbean. They are always walled, but the walls have usually collapsed in places, probably giving the enthusiast a pleasing sense of picturesque decay, but looking to others depressingly unkempt. The pigeon-towers, too, handsome though they look from a distance, are likely to prove half-derelict: and the garden itself, far from being that delicious perfumed retreat of wine and songbird for which the poets had primed us, as often as not looks like a fairly run-down orchard with a kitchen-garden that could do with some weed-killer. Is this, one asks, the Perfection Hafez sings? Is it here that the Persian sages conversed in sweet syllables in their pavilions, while the nightingales sang and the sherbet fizzed?

But the point of the Persian garden, which grows on the stranger as the day wears on, lies not in its form but in its gesture. Its gentle damp shade offers a retort to the voracious desert outside – not a showy retort, nor even defiant, but humorously reproving. It is not so far after all from wasteland to Arcadia: only a step through a gap in the wall, and the ducks and crows which frequent the Persian gardens, dabbling in marble pools or swooping among cypresses, fly or waddle at will from one extreme to the other, reducing both to a proper perspective.

Islam is the State religion. The Muslim conquerors of this country never re-created the glories of her ancient empire, though in the eighteenth century Nadir Shah did march to Delhi and collect the Peacock Throne: but culturally they established another kind of dominion, so that Persian forms and practices spread far to the north and east, and the west began that infatuation with things Persian that has never died.

The Shahanshah himself is a Muslim ruler, but in the past fity years the most vociferous enemies of the throne have often been Muslim activists on the opposite extreme. Either way, Islam can never be ignored in Persia. The Shi'a mullahs thunder about the cities in their green headdresses and swinging cloaks, and off-stage many a successor to the Assassins doubtless cherishes the dream of a Persia dedicated to more ferocious ideals of Islam, where the faith will be enforced by fire or steel, and murder in the cause will be rewarded by certain if not instant transference to Paradise. The great Shi'a shrine at Meshed, a city of domes and courtyards tremendously stacked together in a compound, is the largest landowner in Persia – and is still forbidden to infidels. Islam, which looks so gentle in some flowered country court, can still feel a dangerous creed when the zealot pilgrims glower at you from the gateway of this forbidden sanctuary, the women clutching their black robes, the men glinting their gold teeth.

It feels an immensely forceful creed, too – virile, mystic, with all the irrational exuberance of Lourdes during the pilgrimage, plus elements of brute strength. It is a fine if unnerving experience to pass through Qum, a very holy Persian city, on a Shi'a feast day. Qum is not, like Meshed, tucked well away from infidel inquiry. It is only 90 odd miles south of Tehran, on a well-frequented main road. It is, nevertheless, traditionally among the fiercest Shi'a strongholds in Persia. Here Fatimeh, daughter of the seventh Imam, died in 816, and the shrine above her tomb is a famous place of pilgrimage. Many another holy person is buried round about, and two Islamic theological colleges flood the city with a constant supply of earnest young dogmatics.

It is not sanctity, though, so much as dazzle that strikes the Christian, wandering through this place on a day of Muslim dedication. The streets and squares are jammed with briskly moving pilgrims – city people in blacks and fustian browns, country women from the south in magnificent gypsy petticoats, turbaned grandees, mullahs with staves, all jostling around the bazaar for sacred souvenirs, or pouring in and out of the mosque gates, or seething through the streets, or leaning out of windows talking, laughing, arguing, staring wild-eyed – all on the move, all at full pressure, *urgent*. The noise is indescribable. Through the open gates of the shrine you may see its courtyards blazingly illuminated, with fairy lights and mirrored walls: and when you escape from this vivacious tumult, and cross the river out of town, there behind you the great domes of the mosque stand above the city like reactors, radiating inexhaustible energy, as though their golden tiles are actually glowing with heat, and scattering the fall-out of Islam all over the plateau.

The impact of the modern west upon Persia was no less drastic, and hardly less sudden, than the impact of Islam a thousand years ago – and the west in this context includes Russia to the north. Sixty years ago Persia was the oriental country *par excellence* – very few roads, practically no railways, no modern hotels, women in strict purdah, government mostly by intrigue or antique despotism. People were dressed in all the varied gaiety of the old east, and reaching Tehran from any direction was a proper expedition, involving our ancestors in relays of horses and patent hip-baths. The caravanserai of Persia are now mostly in ruins, and look totally irrelevant to the diesel trucks and buses which roar breakneck down every highway: but there are many people still alive who remember them as busy as airport foyers, the tall camel-caravans stalking through their gateways at sunset, and all the hubbub of victualling, bargaining, gossipping, quarrelling and bedding-down inside.

Victorian Britain and Tsarist Russia were rivals for paramountcy over Persia, until in 1907 they signed a treaty splitting the country into spheres of influence, with a neutral zone in the middle. At each end of Persia these two colossi cast a kind of spell. In the south-east the British, seeping in from their empire in India, established a mesh of consulates and agencies and intrigued themselves into friendship with the powerful nomadic tribes who were all but sovereign in those parts. The friendship went deep. The tribal magnates much attracted the British, who liked their spacious manners and aristocratic field-sport outlook, and felt far more at home with them than with the more devious intelligences of the north. The tribal leaders, for their part, like princes in India, often took to British *mores* in return, sent their sons to school in England, engaged English governesses, and wore very well-cut hacking-jackets. When in 1909 the Anglo-Persian Oil Company was formed to exploit the oil-wells of southern Persia, all that part of the country became more than ever a semi-British fief, so nearly a protectorate that the British Resident at Bushire, on the Persian Gulf, actually had a troop of Indian cavalry to protect him.

In Tehran, too, the British deeply entrenched themselves. British business interests were powerful, British diplomats notoriously influential – sometimes as powers behind the throne, sometimes as agents of liberal reform: in 1906 more than 12,000 Persians, agitators for constitutional change, took refuge in the British Legation compound, a decisive gesture which led to the establishment of a National Assembly and the first Persian Constitution. The British Legation in Tehran was popularly regarded as a very Vatican of secret power. For many years the Imperial Bank of Persia, which until 1930 had the exclusive right to issue bank notes, was actually a British company.

One may still discover relics of this old British presence. Britain was so powerful for so long in Persia that the aura of influence has not yet faded. Old-school Persian gentlemen are still to be seen in old-school English tweeds, and though the British club has long since been internationalized, it still aspires, at least in the minds of elder members, to a Pall Mall dignity and discretion. The occasional English nanny still shows up, pink and bright as ever, at garden parties for the Queen's birthday. The architecture of the Raj is still to be seen at Bushire, in the Anglican church and the old Residency – fives court, panelled ballroom, cavalry lines. The Anglo-Persian Oil Company is no more, but down the Shatt-el-Arab the gigantic refinery at Abadan remains a British memorial of Persepolian proportions, its gardens and avenues nostalgic for Surrey even now, and its club-houses unmistakably descended, if at many removes, from Simla and Ootacamund.

At the other end of Persia the Russians have left far heavier traces. For one thing, they live so near. For another, their armies have far more often marched into Persia (though both sides did so in 1941, amicably meeting in the middle). If the British seemed an insidious sort of threat to Persian sovereignty, working out their ambitions in machination and economic skullduggery, the Russians were far blunter. Three times in this century Russian forces have made armed incursions into Persia. In 1911 the Russians supported an unsuccessful pretender to the throne of the Shahs; after the Second World

War they did their best to detach the province of Azerbaijan from Persia altogether. The neighbouring presence of Russia is inescapable for Persia, and may have significant effects not only on Persian foreign policy, but on social and economic progress.

In the Caspian provinces, over the Elburz, the musty Russian flavour is very strong. You feel it the moment you cross the crest of the mountains, for the Caspian itself lies in the distance grey and sad, and makes you think of lukewarm bortsch and exiles. The countryside up there is not in the least how the world imagines Persia. It is a wet semi-tropical country, sometimes plunged in rainstorms for days at a time. Some of it is green corn country, some looks like Italy, and there are expanses of paddy field and tea-garden which remind me of Ceylon. The peasant houses are often thatched, and are built on stone stilts above the damp. It is a claustrophobic region, hemmed in by the mountains and the sea, with a certain sickroom atmosphere: and Russia is never far away. On the eastern shores of the Caspian you stand on the edge of Russian Asia, looking towards Kazakhstan, towards Bokhara, Samarkand, Tashkent. On the western shores you stand in the approaches to the Caucasus, and the Russians have emphasized the point by studding the frontier with gunposts, watchtowers and radar screens, and lacing it all with television circuits.

From Bandar Pahlevi steamers go up the coast to Baku, in Russia. Once this was the quickest way from Europe to Tehran – train to Baku, ship to Bandar Pahlevi (then called Enzeli), horse or mule across the mountains via Qazvin to Tehran. Now there is not much passenger traffic, but the little port is still pallidly evocative of the old trade, especially on a cold wet day when the wind blusters off the sea. Then the fishermen in their rowing-boats toss miserably about inside the harbour breakwater, and the big white villas along the promenade are sealed with thick brown curtains, as though old ladies from St Petersburg are in there, being served hot chocolate by gossipy maids. It all feels very Russian. On the outskirts of the town, indeed, there is a caviar factory that was actually run by Russians until the 1950s: it has its own retail shop, elaborately *fin-de-siècle*, in which on gleaming marble slabs are displayed not only little tubs of caviar, but chunks of the parent sturgeons too – a shop made for the custom of Grand Duchesses, and the acquisition of Medals of Honour at International Expositions in Kiev.

When Reza Shah decided to modernize his Caspian shoreline, and turn part of it into a resort area, he modelled its new towns to Russian colonial patterns – pompous in the centre, fustian around the edges. A room in a small hotel in any of these little places – Lissar, say, or Lahijan – pungently brings home to the visitor the proximity of Russia. We climb some very steep and narrow steps to reach it, the porter wheezing with our bags behind, and find it to be almost solid with the heat and fumes of its paraffin stove, as though we are enduring the depths of a Moscow winter. It is decorated overwhelmingly in blues and browns. Brown velvet curtains shroud the window. A thick brown

31

shagreen cloth covers the table, with brown bobbles all around. The door is bright blue, and so is the ceiling, and there is a hatstand with blue plastic knobs. The beds are very brass, with baubles and quilt mattresses, and inside the wardrobe are neatly laid out a towel, a brush and a blue comb. And when, with a very gentle knock on the door, the servant arrives with your dinner, you find it to be laid with a truly Russian lavishness upon a spotless white cloth: lamb, rice, bread, salad, sour milk, lemonade, black tea. The servant gives the paraffin stove a shake, to hasten the asphyxiation, and leaves you with a serfly bow: but as you eat your dinner you can hear his stertorous breath outside your door, very close to the latch, in case some whim of yours requires his respectful attention.

Another kind of reminder is to be found at the port of Bandar Shah, along the Caspian coast. There Reza Shah built the eastern terminal of his Trans-Iranian Railway, but even this great patriotic venture was given a Russian seal. During the Second World War the line became the chief Anglo-American supply route to Russia, by which arms and stores were shipped to the Russian armies in the Caucasus. Today, if you look over the wall beside the railway station, you may see a melancholy parade of the locomotives that hauled this historic traffic – rusty old engines from American foundries, boiler to boiler, slowly subsiding on their driving wheels, but still able to suggest the times when their passage across the Persian plateau linked one war-front with another. What mighty Powers they connected, in their snorting hissing days! How aloofly important they must

VI Kurdish women

Westernization has introduced a drab uniformity into the dress of Persian town dwellers, among whom only some women and girls with their all-enveloping *chadors* (see Plate 29) provide a distinctive Persian touch. But among the nomadic and semi-nomadic tribal people – Kurds, Lurs, Bakhtiaris, Qashqais, Afshars, Turkomens, Arabs, Baluchis, etc. – hitherto relatively remote from the westernizing influences of the towns, traditional tribal dress is still much worn, particularly by women.

This photograph was taken in north-western Azerbaijan near the ancient Armenian church of St Thaddeus (Plate VII) in a Kurdish village when a wedding was being celebrated. The whole village was *en fête* and everyone dressed in their best for the occasion.

Note the tattoo mark on the chin of one of the women; such marks, used for the adornment of the female face, are fairly common among some of the tribes of Persia. The pyramids in the background have been built up of round pats of sun-dried cattle dung which is extensively used as fuel in this and other parts of Asia where there is a shortage of timber.

VII West Azerbaijan Province, Church of St Thaddeus

The Armenian church and monastery of St Thaddeus, known locally by the Turkish name of Kara Kilisa (Black Church), is situated in desolate, but nowadays easily accessible, country about 13 miles south of Maku, close to the Turkish border, in what was once part of the ancient Kingdom of Armenia.

According to Armenian legend, the Apostle Thaddeus (generally identified as St Jude) reached this corner of Armenia about AD 66 and built there the world's first church; he was later martyred and buried in his own church. The present cruciform building, said to be on the site of this early church, stands on a hill within fortified walls and consists of two distinct parts – a domed sanctuary end (Plate 70) built largely of dark stone, probably dating from the 10th or 11th century, and the main body of the church, built of light sandstone, under a second and larger tent dome whose twelve-sided drum is pierced by an equal number of windows. According to an inscription dated 1329 this latter section was rebuilt after an earthquake in 1319; considerable additions were, however, made during the 19th century, possibly when there was an abortive move to transfer here from Echmiadzin in Russia the seat of the Armenian Catholicos.

The exterior walls are, like those of other early Armenian churches, decorated with bas-reliefs, the effigies of saints and a lively frieze of vine leaves and animals on the newer building being particularly striking. Ruined buildings within a walled compound adjoining the western fortified walls indicate that a considerable monastic settlement once existed there.

VIII Sultaniyeh, mausoleum of Oljeitu Khodabana

Situated 25 miles south-east of Zanjan, the half-way town between Tehran and Tabriz, this huge mausoleum, regarded by Sir Roger Stevens (British Ambassador to Iran, 1954–58, and author of *The Land of the Great Sophy*, an admirable book about Persia and its antiquities) as 'the most astounding building in Persia', is all that remains of the great walled city built between 1305 and 1313 by the Mongol Ilkhan Oljeitu Khodabana, who transferred his capital there from Tabriz and named it Sultaniyeh, *i.e.* Imperial.

The mausoleum, designed in the first place for himself, towers over the flat-roofed village below. It is built of brick and was partly faced, both inside and out, with coloured tile-work, of which traces remain. The inner walls were originally of light-coloured brick decorated with small dark blue tiles, but in 1313 they were covered with plaster, and then painted with medallions, floral designs and Koranic inscriptions. An open arcaded gallery, whose vaults are attractively decorated with plaster-faced brick, runs round the building below a stalactite cornice.

Oljeitu, who was converted to Shi'ism in 1309 (but later lapsed back to Sunnism) and must have been conscious that the site of his new capital was not well chosen from a communications point of view, at one time thought of remedying this deficiency by turning Sultaniyeh into a great Shi'ite pilgrim centre. (See also Plate 63.)

have seemed, as they sped from the American ships on the Persian Gulf to the Russian ships on the Caspian! How telling a commentary they still provide, even abandoned on their quay, upon Persia's place in the contemporary world! They make this long-fallen empire feel no more than incidental to the cataclysmic events that occur beyond her frontiers, and send one back across the mountains with a sense of heady escape: for it is a long, long way from Bandar Shah to the delights of inner Persia.

Inner Persia: yet so strong is the character of that inner country, the tang and irony of Persia, that almost everything it touches is in some way transformed, however alien its origins and purposes. A taxi-driver at Resht, overtaking me with difficulty one day on the Ramsar road, looked at me furiously as he passed, and blew his horn in solemn protest. It made a noise like a cow mooing, very realistically – and I wondered how its distant inventor, in some far-off Novelty Fun Factory of the west, would respond to this dis-tinctly unfrivolous employment of his jape. The Persian pulse beats erratically, and some-how gives to every Persian activity an unexpected twist, making almost every aspect of this extraordinary country not *merely* extraordinary, but actually unique. Let us con-sider, from the whole wide spectrum of the national life, three widely disconnected subjects: buses, food, horse fairs.

Buses first, the caravans of modern Persia. In other places the country bus is often a comical vehicle, bent in the middle in Egypt, or pottering steamed with gossip from village to village in the Cotswolds. Not the Persian kind. It is likely to be a very large and modern German bus, flamingly painted and covered with self-advertisement (*Two Luce* and *Doo Lows* are only two of many Persian approximations to *De Luxe*). It keeps up a staggering average speed, trailing dust and diesel smoke far behind it, and when it reaches a teashop, in it swings with a flamboyant screech of tyres and blast of triple horns, and out tumble all its jam-packed passengers, to stretch themselves, grab a bowl of stew or queue for the outdoor lavatories. In the big cities, late at night, one often glimpses the buses gleaming through the arches of courtyards, with men strapping luggage on their roofs, and passengers milling all about in the dim streetlight, waiting to start on some midnight marathon. In Isfahan they wash the buses beneath the arches of the bridge called Pul-e-Allah Verdi Khan, into which, up to their hocks in the Zaindeh river, they almost exactly fit.

Most of Persia travels by bus. I once came across a big Mercedes *Doo Lows* stuck in soft sand, its back wheels spinning helplessly and its driver beginning to look distraught. Several cars and lorries had stopped to give a hand. We heaved and sweated in the heat, but were simply not strong enough, and presently the driver got out of his cab, came back to have a look, and visibly reached a reluctant decision. He poked his head through the door and asked his passengers to help: and out there came, looking displeased and stretching their arms as though interrupted in deep sleep, what seemed to be a battalion of Persian paratroopers, crew-cut and strong as horses. They looked at us resentfully, put their great shoulders to the chassis and had the bus out in a moment: and I saw the driver ushering them inside again with apologies as the rest of us, shambled and forlorn, resumed our interrupted journeys.

Food next. This is, to the westerner, very surprising. Persia's gift of adaptation has never been uncritical – the patterns and standards that she has accepted from the outside world have generally been refined to her own taste, deprived of fat and ornament, purified. This is well demonstrated in her victuals. She shares many ingredients and basic recipes with her neighbours, but she eats differently from anyone else. Take the national dish of *chelau kebab*. *Kebab* as the Turks or Egyptians serve it is a crude if satisfying dish – chunks of lamb stuck on a skewer and roasted over charcoal. *Chelau kebab*, as the Persians eat it, is something very different. It is lamb too, but a strip of lamb, beaten thin and tender, and laid upon a bed of exceedingly dry white rice from the Caspian. This simple centre-piece is the basis of a most sophisticated meal. A raw egg is beaten into the rice to give it richness, and around it is arranged a variety of salads: raw onions always, and in season splendidly crisp cos lettuce, together with nasturtiums, cresses, radishes, gherkins, and all manner of unidentified herbs and grasses, which seem to have been picked five minutes before in the next-door meadow, and give you a fine organic boost.

The unleavened bread of Persia is delicious: it comes, they say, in at least forty varieties, nearly every town having a different way of making it. The butter is as good as any I know, except only the butter of Caernarvonshire, and Persian fruits are famous: melons from the Isfahan oasis, apples and pears, oranges from Shiraz or the Caspian littoral, pome-granates, grapes and that most Persian of all fruits, the peach – which originated in this country, so some botanists believe, and entered Europe with the armies of the Achae-menians. Milk is generally drunk sour, as yoghourt or buttermilk, often with little bits of onion in it, or herbs, or soda-water: rice is imaginatively dressed up in a score of dishes, with orange peel, with carrots, with almonds, with herbs, with beans or cinnamon, with eggs and pieces of chicken. Truck-drivers at drive-ins stock up with superb hot stews, thickened with mutton, and sometimes elevated by duck, crushed walnuts, onion, cinnamon and pomegranate juice to form one of the most memorable dishes of the east. The scruffiest roadside teahouse, torn oilcloth on its tables and corrugated iron on its roof, will whistle you up a glass of excellent hot tea: and at another extreme Persian caviar is said by those who know everything to be the best in the world.

A Persian greengrocers' is a sight to see – a revelation that must have intoxicated the first Arab invaders out of the desert. The greenstuffs drip and sprawl all over the place, fronds of feathery herbs, swathes of root vegetables, luscious lettuces still flaked with soil, rising in tiers of green and wholesome nourishment beside the dusty sidewalk. Finally there are the wines, which have been legendary for centuries. Wine is forbidden to Muslims, but the Persians have never been altogether denied it. There has always been some infidel minority to grow it for them: some have defiantly continued to grow it for themselves. Jews, Armenians and the surviving Zoroastrians are the principal growers now, and Julfa, the Armenian quarter of Isfahan, has long played the part of a communal speak-easy. In Shiraz they still produce the thick and heady red wine so dear to the Persian poets, but the best wines now come from further north—notably from Qazvin, whose wine was described by Chardin as being '*le plus violent du monde et aussi le plus delicieux*' (though nowadays it is not so violent as the sometimes explosive Persian soda-water). Persia, you see, is not one of your dried-up sand states, lubricated only by its crude oil. People here do not simply eat and drink to live. Life, though seldom lavish, is generous enough to allow some hedonism in the kitchen, and as a matter of fact the fragile and and sensitive salads of the country, disposed with such delicacy on your table, seem to me almost the last popular expression of Persia's traditional genius for form.

The buses – boisterous: the food – one might say sensual: the horse fairs – but when I speak of horse fairs, I have a particular fair in mind, like no other I know. Discussing one day the tall poignant Rosinantes, knock-kneed and patrician, so often to be seen pulling carts and gharries around the Persian towns, I asked an acquaintance where I could best see the more stalwart Turkomen horses of the north. 'Pahlevi Dej', he replied at once, 'Thursday morning before breakfast' – and there and then I went. It is a village in the Gorgan steppes, not far from the Dome of Qabus, and each week the Yamut Turko-men tribes of the area hold a trading fair. Many of these people are settled in villages now, but many more still wander the open steppe with their portable round houses, like igloos of thatch and felt: and in ones and twos on Thursday morning they converge upon Pahlevi Dej, bolt upright on their horses, top-heavy in their black fleece hats, in stately lolloping motion across their magnificent landscape. Some bring their wives with them, demurely riding pillion, and wearing purple or scarlet skirts and brightly flowered shawls: and sometimes a visitor waylays a Turkomen on the way to market, crouching with camera and exposure meter to catch a picture as he passes – but not for a moment does the pace flag, inexorably the horseman continues his progress, kicking up little clouds of dust with each step, and looking distantly down from the saddle as through a thick glass plate.

These are the most daunting of the Persian peoples. Brown, slant-eyed, thin-lipped, their faces often fringed with white beard, they look as though nothing is beyond their powers, noble or atrocious, as though they never betrayed a panic or revealed a secret in their lives. Their horse fair is conducted with a reticent calm worthy of Fortnums in its heyday. In the livestock yard a solitary horseman trots his grey imperially through the crowd, head held high, eyes flickering right and left, with a brown cloak slung over his shoulders and a rich red carpet-cloth beneath his saddle. He is only hoping to sell his horse, but looks as though he is about to represent his people at a coronation. Here a recalcitrant goat is disciplined by a strong brown hand around a horn; here a pair of shepherds, locked in negotiation, stand in absolute silence face to face, each avoiding the other's eye, until the hint of a nod or the suspicion of a tossed head takes the bargaining a stage further. A man lifts a ewe in his arms to judge her weight. Two formidable youths sit motionless upon their ponies, taking no notice of anybody at all, but looking as though one misplaced word or gesture might seal your fate most uncomfortably.

Kebab is roasting on the pavement, and its hot spiced smell permeates the fair. In the carpet-yard the tribal carpets lie in heaps, reds and greens blazing in the dust. In the village streets men stand talking in undertones on the pavement, like ranch-hands in some threatened cow-town of the American West. When the fair ends the horsemen pack up their belongings silently and disperse without haste across the plains, their tall humped figures scattering across the skyline in lordly independence. It is in many ways a theatrical occasion, the horse fair at Pahlevi Dej: but then few events in Persia, however prosaic in the theory, are without a spice of drama in the act.

The extraordinary is still the commonplace in this country, but it is no use pretending that the genius of the Persians has flowered in the twentieth century as it always did. Today the genius of the Persians, as we of the outside world cherish it, seldom flowers at all. Exquisite carpets are still made, but generally to antique patterns. Skilful miniatures are painted, but they are more craft than art. The architecture of modern Persia has gener-ally been of stunning banality, and scarcely a beautiful building has been erected for a century. Persian attention to aesthetics is aptly illustrated by the duty of a policeman who stands beside the gateway at Persepolis, immediately beneath the great platform: it is his job, diligently performed, to ensure that every arriving vehicle is parked the same way round—not to avoid congestion or inconvenience, but only to keep the scene, by order, properly symmetrical.

This is a taint of the west. The latest of Persia's invaders have been the most damaging. Ever since the Arab invasion the Persians have intermittently thought of themselves as a great people gone down in the world; but it was only in the nineteenth century, I think, that their old conviction of innate superiority began to flag, and they began to feel them-selves backward or shamefully unmechanized. It was the example of the new industrial Europe that gave them this complex, and by the 1920s travellers from the west had to be distinctly careful what they said, in case it should be thought contemptuous. An inflammatory combination had been fused, between the pride of a civilization 2,500 years old, and the doubts of a people patently overtaken in the world.

Reza Shah, like many another Asian and African ruler, decided that resistance to west-ern values was useless, and boldly set about remoulding Persia to a new image. Like

Attaturk in Turkey, he wanted to create a secular state freed of its historical and religious inhibitions: and around you, wherever you look in Persia today, his monuments remain. He stripped the men of their silken robes and the women of their black enveloping *chadors*. He attacked the power of the mullahs, he abolished titles of nobility, he made a start with the education of the poor, he built the Trans-Iranian Railway. He threw wide boulevards through the ancient tumble of the Persian cities, to the discomfiture of the architectural purists and the wondering delight of the inhabitants. He vastly weakened the power of the great tribal leaders, and all over the southern country to this day armed sentries stand guard outside the little white forts, topped by gigantic flags, which keep an eye on the tribes – stiffening themselves into ceremonial salute for every car that passes. Reza Shah, like him or not, will be remembered as powerfully as Abbas the Great, if not Darius himself.

His revolution is not ended yet. Persia remains recognizably an oriental country, and the western culture is still not altogether acclimatized. Nothing brings out the dichotomy more clearly than the Motor-Car, that universal agent of change, which reveals the condition of communities no less vividly than the character of individuals. It is an agreeable surprise that the Motor-Car has not yet succeeded in destroying the old courtesy of the Persians. This has always been a people of beautiful manners. The convivial hospitality of the Persians captivated nearly all their early western visitors, and every memoir records their bonhomie – 'courteous, friendly towards foreigners and tractable', 'conversible Good Fellows, sparing no one the Bowl in their turn', 'the zone they live in makes them tawny, the wine cheerful, the opium salacious'. These pleasant characteristics survive even the motor age. The traffic of Tehran is perhaps the most desperate in the world – traffic sufficient, it seems, to keep a whole continent on the move, driven with a hair-raising air of incompetent insouciance: yet even through this diurnal chaos the charm of the Persians impenitently shows – with a cheery wave of the hand your informant zig-zags across the passage of a double-decker bus, through a red light and up a no-entry street, to deposit you most kindly at the back door of the wrong museum after closing time. If your car breaks down on a desert road, do not despond: the next truck-driver and his mate are sure to help you, showing themselves in repose far gentler than you might suppose from their furious momentum in action, blowing the dirt out of your carburettor with gracious condescension, and probably refusing to accept a penny for their pains – until, with a ghastly roar of their exhaust, they leap away into the desert again jammed tight in their cab, hands waving from all windows.

But the Motor-Car, which isolates a man from his fellows, and denies him the solaces of tradition and convention, demonstrates also a certain poignancy to the Persian condition – a half-way state, a transient state, in which a whole nation is slowly shifting cultures. I was once stuck for a few hours in a blizzard on one of the Elburz passes, between the

Caspian and Tehran. There were fifteen or twenty cars and buses in the same predicament, and it was interesting to see how the emancipated Persians, most of them born into the era of Reza Shah, responded to an essentially modern or mechanical emergency. Bogged down as we all were in the snow, several archetypes of a changing Persia were etched on my memory, together with their several reactions.

There was a schoolmaster, bespectacled, liberal, Anglophile, with his plain sensible wife in his family car – just that figure of the educated middle classes every development economist loves to meet. There was a feudal magnate, deep in the back seat of a Mercedes, whose hook nose and dark-rimmed eyes sometimes peered out in a disparaging way at gathering snowdrifts, as if to imply that they would never have happened in the old days. There was a stout army officer in uniform and mackintosh, surely a major-general at least, with a beautiful wife about half his age, broad in the beam and headscarfed, and two small girls in pink tights. There was an American-trained helicopter pilot, Sikorskis on his tie, *Time* on his back seat, Kleenex in the glove compartment and a wife in scarlet earmuffs. There were four or five goodnatured miscellaneous families, joking, eating sandwiches or getting out to throw snowballs at each other: and there were half a dozen bus-drivers, big boorish men in dark glasses, leaning morosely on their driving wheels and picking their teeth.

When the confused exertions of a snowplough churned a passage through the snow, all these characters were prodded into action and thrown into relief. Traffic from the other side bore down uncontrolled upon the half-cleared passage, the pass was thrown into tumult, and the Persians were obliged to react. One could see the centuries in conflict up there. The helicopter pilot, consulting his watch, his map and his wife, surveyed the mounting confusion in front of us, skilfully turned his car around, and disappeared towards the Caspian. The magnate simply sank deeper into his seat and dispatched his chauffeur, with a duster over his head, trudging through the snow to see what was happening. The general stepped out of his car in person to take a look at things for himself: but finding it very wet outside, he turned back after a moment or two and handed his uniform cap to his wife, lest the damp should tarnish the gold braid. The schoolmaster came and talked to me: the police had assured him the road would soon be clear, but he wondered all the same – though on the other hand – it was true that – it might be a good idea to – but perhaps all in all it would be best to wait and see. The miscellaneous families lost some of their patience, and took to floundering about in the drifts, getting their back wheels stuck in ruts, and kicking up snow all over the place. The four bus-drivers unanimously launched their mighty vehicles in front of us all, spraying everyone with snow and ice, lurching and skidding hugely through the blizzard, until at last, one after the other, they came to a squashy halt in the middle of the pass, entirely blocking it all over again, and condemning us all to another two hours' wait.

It seemed to me an allegorical confusion, for the old civilization of this country was so complex, and so subtle, that its gradual westernization has been a traumatic experience for the nation. Lives have been twisted, flung about, re-moulded. Values have been re-assessed, traditions re-examined. A generation ago (I thought to myself) that Mercedes magnate probably ruled an estate the size of an English county with an authority almost absolute. My friend the schoolmaster, so hamstrung by all the liberal hesitations, was the son of a poor Government clerk, a hubble-bubble man, numbly doing what he was told, and only allowing himself a grain or two of opium on holiday evenings. The general's father was a sergeant, who rose high in rank and urbanity, bequeathing to his son the wherewithal for a lovely young wife, and all the military virtues. The helicopter man was born in a domed mud house on the edge of the desert, ten miles from a paved road, fifty miles from a doctor, five hundred miles from an airfield.

The four bus-drivers graduated direct, I have no doubt, from the mule-train.

Reza Shah's reform movement was essentially an importation of ideas and standards – a westernization of an eastern country. Though it is not yet completed, it has already over-lapped another, more fundamental revolution: the White or Bloodless Revolution, whose impetus now keeps the country in a ferment of change and excitement. Persia

IX Qum, shrine of Fatimeh the Immaculate (shrine of Hasrat-e-Ma'sumeh). North façade

Fatimeh is said to have died in Qum in AD 816 when on her way to Meshed to visit her brother, the Eighth Imam. Her shrine is second only to her brother's at Meshed (Plate X), as a Shi'ite pilgrimage centre in Persia. But it was not until Shi'ism became the official religion of Persia under the Safavids, and Shah Ismail (1499–1524) built a sanctuary over her tomb, that Qum became the major pilgrim centre which it remains today. The Qajar monarchs, Fath Ali Shah (1791–1834) and Nasr-ud-din Shah (1848–96), embellished the shrine – the former adding the gold-plated copper tiles to its main dome and the latter the gold stalactites at the far end of the *ivan*. The dazzling mirror work in the entrance portal also dates from Qajar times.

The religious fanaticism for which Qum has long been notorious is lessening, though non-Moslems are still forbidden entrance to the shrine and its precincts, where three Safavid Shahs – Safi (d. 1641), Abbas II (d. 1668) and Suleiman (d. 1694) – and the bearded Qajar Shah, Fath Ali, reputed father of over a hundred children, are buried.

Qum, which lies about 90 miles south of Tehran on the north-western edge of the formidable Dasht-e-Kavir, the Great Salt Desert, is also known for its pottery, its high quality carpets and a thin wafer-like sweet, *sohan*, resembling butterscotch.

now understands well enough the material techniques of the west, which are a *sine qua non* of national independence. She has expelled those alien interests, economic or political, which once dominated her affairs. Though she is a military ally of the United States and Great Britain, she has close relations with Russia too, and conforms slavishly to no *bloc* or international lobby. Having re-established her identity, now she is trying to rejuvenate herself – socially, educationally, spiritually even.

The powerhouse of this movement is Tehran, and its chief engineer is the Shahan-shah, the King of Kings. For anyone interested in history in its richest sense, there is more to learn in Tehran today than in Isfahan or Persepolis. Here the Pahlevi dynasty, the latest of the royal Persian lines, has concentrated its power and established its presence. If one must go to Naqsh-e-Rustam to catch the shadow of Xerxes, in Tehran you are never far from the splendour of Mohammed Reza Shah Pahlevi, whose several palaces form a focus for this city, whose audiences and gracious visits dominate the newspapers, whose photograph hangs in nearly every shop, whose plans for the regeneration of his country find their place in every guidebook, whose face everyone knows, whose views on the future of the Persian Gulf are anxiously weighed in Chanceries, who crowned himself at his own coronation, whose predecessors were Cambyses and Tamerlane, and whose dominions range from Maku to Saravan.

In Tehran the envoys, craftsmen and traders of all nations reside, as once they settled in the ateliers and caravanserai of Isfahan. Russian engineers report progress on new steel mills, American technicians drive dusty into town from their microwave stations on the Shiraz road, British archaeologists present their findings to the museum authorities. Jets scream over the city. Tehran is a great staging post on the round-the-world routes, and exotically uniformed air crews from many nations check in day and night at the city's hotels. The old Silk Route has become part of the Trans-Asia highway, which will one

X Meshed, shrine of the Imam Reza, the Chamber of
Salutation (Dar-ol-Salaam)

This inner chamber, deep within the shrine, is decorated with newly-fitted mirror work which glitters like silver in the brilliant tungsten light. The floor and dado, as well as the balustrade in the foreground, are made of a local yellow marble.

Pilgrims pass from the Chamber of Salutation into the holy of holies, the *Haram*, or tomb chamber of the Eighth Imam. Three doors lead into the *Haram* – one of silver given by Nadir Shah, another of gold plate studded with jewels given by Fath Ali Shah and a third also of gold plate. A dado of early 13th-century Kashan lustre tiles lines the tomb chamber. (See also Plates 87–92.)

45

day link Europe with the Far East, and already coaches from London and Munich regularly arrive in the city.

Tehran is the greatest of the Persian markets. Squat and black in the heart of the city, like a covered railway station, stand the bazaars – oriental bazaars still, not quite emasculated yet, for all the rubber sandals from Hong Kong and plastic bags stamped with the initials of totally imaginary airlines. Down there you may still smell the spices and the sheepskins, and hear the rich *frump, frump* of unrolling carpets, unpeeled from the stack like pages of a manuscript. All the faces of Persia may be seen in those arcades, Semite or Mongol, fair or swarthy, swathed in fringed turbans or clamped upon by dowdy trilbies. It is an imperial sort of place: Darius would have liked it.

And Tehran retains, for all its brashness, noise and wealth, a magical obscurity. It sparkles with quirk and lesser mystery – door numbers of no logic, huge highways inexplicably deserted, coincidences, riddles. It is not at all a simple or an obvious capital. Pictures may show its power and ugliness, descriptions may capture some of its wit: but its tangy strangeness only experience can convey – when the watchmen's fires blaze in the streets of the capital at midnight, when the little streaky carp on the roadside stalls swim round and round in the neon-light, or the great wall of the Elburz stands preternaturally sharp above Tehran, as though its line of peaks has been touched up in the studio, or over-exposed.

This vibrant city is the setting of the White Revolution: for this revolution, far more than Reza Shah's, is fundamentally *Persian*. It has been launched, by a fine Persian paradox, under the auspices of the Crown in one of the world's most active monarchies. Its epithet is aptly chosen, for it is certainly anything but Red. The Shah himself is its chief advocate. Its reforms have been radical: the re-distribution of land, the emancipation of women, the education of an illiterate peasantry. Among ordinary people there is, I am assured, a new spirit of hope and confidence abroad. Certainly there is a stimulating sense of motion, as fine new roads leap across the countryside, as mills and schools and power stations everywhere arise, as the cars fill the city streets at rush-hour, and the apartment blocks of the new middle class tower above the suburbs. There are few countries where the radical energies seem to be burning more furiously.

This is not quite the standard revolution of rising expectations, so dear to the economic theorists. It is true that expectancy in Persia, from expectancy of life to expectancy of car ownership, has lately boomed: but Persia is not one of those many ancient states which must be pumped into economic take-off. This revolution is being achieved for the most part by indigenous wealth and vigour, and by the leadership of the second of the Pahlevis. Just as Persia was never part of a modern fructifying empire, British, French or Russian, so she is not today one of your wards of the rich. She is using, as always, foreign resources and talents, but she is marshalling them to a particularly Persian rhythm, to an altogether

Persian order. It cannot be said that the country is being Americanized, or Russianized, or even westernized in quite Reza Shah's sense. Though the new artifacts of Persia conform to the general international monotony, and the Rotarians meet here as purposefully as anywhere else, still the particular pungency of Persian society has not been destroyed. There is still a spiced, or possibly acrid, scent to the air.

Foreign money pours into Persia today. Visiting newspapermen write laudatory columns. Ambassadors glow with respect. Trade missions fawn. The Shahanshah, as I write, is handsomely in command of his affairs, and the Pahlevis stand majestically in the line of the Qajars, the Safavids, the Timurids, the Seljuks, the Sassanians, the Seleucids and the Achaemenians themselves – emperors all, and reformers too, in one kind or another, in their day.

No envoi? None: not because the denouement of these events is still unknown, but because Persia is herself an inconclusive spirit, where nothing is final—where sand only covers sand, dynasties slide into dynasties, and a descriptive essay seems to demand less a peroration, or even a last aphorism, than some delicate asymmetrical device beneath the text, or a pressed flower to introduce the pictures.

JAMES MORRIS

BIBLIOGRAPHY

Arberry, A. J. *The Legacy of Persia,* Oxford 1953
Arfa, Hassan *The Kurds,* Oxford 1966

Bell, Gertrude *Earlier Letters,* London, New York 1937
  Persian Pictures, London 1947
Blunt, Wilfred *Pietro's Pilgrimage,* London 1953
Blunt, Wilfred and Swann, W. *Isfahan,* New York 1966
Browne, E. G. *A Literary History of Persia,* London 1906
  The Persian Revolution, Cambridge 1910, New York 1966
Byron, Robert *The Road to Oxiana,* London, Mystic, Conn., 1937

Cameron, George, D. *Archaeology,* vol. 13, no. 13, New York 1960
Carswell, John *New Julfa,* Oxford 1968
Churchill, Winston S. *The Second World War,* vol. v, London 1951
Costa, A. and Lockhart, L. *Persia,* London 1937
Creswell, K. A. C. *Early Muslim Architecture,* Harmondsworth 1958
Curzon, G. N. *Persia and the Persian Question,* London 1892, New York 1966

Edwards, A. C. *The Persian Carpet,* London 1953

Ghirshman, Roman *Iran : Parthians and Sassanians,* London 1962
  Iran from the Earliest Times to the Islamic Conquest, Harmondsworrh 1954
  Mémoires de la Délégation Archaéologique en Iran : Tchoga Zanbil, vol. I, Paris 1966

Godard, André *The Art of Iran,* London, New York 1965

Hall, Melvin *Journey to the End of an Era,* New York 1947
Herodotus *The Histories,* Harmondsworth 1954, New York 1964
Herzfeld, Ernst *Iran in the Ancient East,* Oxford 1941
Hill, Derek and Grabar, A. *Islamic Architecture and its Decoration,* London, Chicago 1964

Ibn Battuta *Travels,* London 1928
Iran, Journal of the British Institute of Persian Studies, vols. I–IV, 1963–66 (Articles by E. Beazley and D. Stronach)
Iran Almanac, Tehran 1968

Kazemaini, K. and Babayan, S. S. *Zoorkhaneh or Gymnasium,* Tehran 1964
Kleiss, Wolfram *Istanbuler Mitteilungen,* German Archaeological Institute, vol. 17, 1967

Le Strange, G. *The Lands of the Eastern Caliphate,* Cambridge 1930, New York 1905
Levy, Reuben *Persian Literature,* Oxford 1923
Lockhart, Laurence *Persian Cities,* London 1960

Pahlavi, Mohammed Reza Shah *Mission for my Country,* London 1961
Pope, A. Upham *A Survey of Persian Art,* 6 vols., Oxford 1938–39
   Persian Architecture, London, New York 1965
Porada, Edith *Ancient Iran,* London 1962

Sackville-West, V. *Passenger to Tehran,* London 1926
Sami, Ali *Pasargadae,* Shiraz 1956
   Persepolis, Shiraz 1958
   Shiraz, Shiraz 1958
Schmidt, E. F. *Persepolis I,* Chicago 1953
Stevens, Roger *The Land of the Great Sophy,* London 1962
Stronach, David *Journal of Near Eastern Studies,* vols. 25 and 26, Chicago 1966–67
Sykes, Percy *A History of Persia,* 2 vols., London 1915

Walser, G. *Die Völkerschaften auf den Reliefs vom Persepolis,* Berlin 1966
Wilber, Donald H. *Persian Gardens and Pavilions,* Tokyo 1962
Wills, C. J. *In the Land of the Lion and Sun,* London 1891
Wulff, Hans E. *The Traditional Crafts of Persia,* Cambridge, Mass. 1966

Part One   CLASSICAL PERSIA

16

17

18

20

21

1 PASARGADAE, TOMB OF CYRUS THE GREAT. DAYBREAK

In 550 BC Cyrus II, King of Parsa in the south-west of present-day Persia, overthrew his overlord and grandfather, King Astyages of Media, thus establishing the Achaemenian dynasty (named after his ancestor Achaemenes, founder of the family's fortunes) as rulers of the combined Kingdoms of the Medes and the Persians. Herodotus records how, through subsequent conquests, Cyrus and his successors, Cambyses II, Darius and Xerxes, created the first world empire of antiquity with frontiers stretching from the Nile to the Oxus, the Aegean to the Indus.

The Achaemenian Empire's first capital was built by Cyrus (559–530 BC) at Pasargadae, in a beautiful mountain valley about 25 miles as the crow flies north-east of Persepolis, chosen according to one tradition because it was near the site of his victory over Astyages. It was at Pasargadae, too, that Cyrus's modest but well-sited tomb was built during his lifetime. It is made of large blocks of white limestone, is nearly 35 ft. high, and consists of a high plinth of six receding steps crowned by a gabled tomb chamber. Though there is little doubt about the identity of the tomb, no trace survives of the inscription mentioned by various classic writers and recorded by Strabo as 'O Man, I am Cyrus, who founded the Empire of the Persians and was King of Asia. Grudge me not therefore this monument'.

The tomb is locally known as that of the Mother of Solomon. In the thirteenth century it was enclosed by a mosque built from the ancient stones of Pasargadae, of which the gateway shown in the photograph still stands.

2 PASARGADAE, CYRUS THE GREAT'S AUDIENCE HALL

Among the scattered Achaemenian ruins of Cyrus the Great's first capital the Audience Hall is one of three structures within what is known as the palace area, the other two being the Gatehouse (the least well preserved) and the Residential Palace.

The first excavations at Pasargadae were undertaken by the German archaeologist, Professor E. Herzfeld, in 1928, but it was not until 1950 that the entire ground-plan of the Audience Hall was uncovered by Iranian archaeologists working under Mr Ali Sami, then Director of the Archaeological Institute of Persepolis. This revealed within an area 230 by 130 ft. a rectangular central hall (111 by 72 ft.), whose ceiling was supported by two rows of four columns, while a roofed colonnade ran round its four sides. The floor of the hall was paved with well-cut and polished slabs of white limestone laid on a foundation of rougher stone. A single 36 ft. column still stands. Unlike the buildings at Persepolis, which were square, those at Pasargadae were rectangular; another unusual feature was the skilful use made of contrasting white and black limestone.

The most recent excavations at Pasargadae were those of the British Institute of Persian Studies in 1961–63 under the direction of Mr David Stronach, in the course of which a rich treasure of Achaemenian gold and silver jewellery was found.

3 PASARGADAE, CYRUS'S RESIDENTIAL PALACE

The remains of this palace, with its central hall of thirty columns, lies 250 yards to the north of Cyrus's Audience Hall (Plate 2), and have all that building's distinguishing features. The unfluted white columns (cf. the fluted dark grey limestone columns of Persepolis) had a finely moulded base of seven concentric rings, and stood on a three-tier pedestal, the bottom tier being of black stone in contrast to the white of the rest. Unfortunately, no trace of any capitals from these columns has been found.

Sami, who excavated the larger part of this palace in 1950–51, believes that, because the doorways were so much narrower than those of the Audience Hall, this must have been the private residence of Cyrus. Other archaeologists are less certain and refer to it as 'the northern palace'.

4 NAQSH-E-RUSTAM, KA'BA ZARDUSHT (THE CUBE OF ZOROASTER)

This well-preserved and nicely proportioned (38 ft. high by 23 ft. 9 in. square) building faces the royal Achaemenian rock tombs at Naqsh-e-Rustam, five miles north of Persepolis. There is a very similar though greatly ruined structure at Pasargadae, known as Zendan-e-Suleiman (Solomon's Prison). After nearly a hundred years of controversy, experts are still arguing over the purpose these two buildings served. Some, like Curzon and Herzfeld, consider they were royal tombs; others, like Ghirshman, fire temples; yet others that they were royal embalming chambers or depositories for the royal standards. Recently Stronach has drawn attention to the architectural parallels between newly discovered Urartian tower temples in south-east Turkey and these two Achaemenian structures, thus tipping the scales in favour of the temple theory.

The Ka'ba is built of large blocks of finely dressed white limestone. The only opening is an elegant doorway at the head of a flight of stone steps opposite Artaxerxes I's tomb. Each of the outer walls is decorated with rows of vertical slots cut in the limestone; additionally, all but the door-wall are embellished with six recessed dummy windows of black basalt. There is a single chamber inside with a lofty ceiling spanned by four vast stones. The external walls bear inscriptions from Sassanian times, of which one, in

Sassanian, Parthian and Greek, records the struggle between the Sassanian and Roman Empires.

5, 6 NAQSH-E-RUSTAM, SASSANIAN BAS-RELIEFS

The early Sassanian kings sought to emphasize their claim to be the descendants and successors of the Achaemenians (who, like themselves, came from Fars and were of Persian blood) by carving eight great bas-reliefs on the rock face where the Achaemenian kings were buried, some of them immediately below the royal tombs. They date from the third and early fourth centuries and, like other Sassanian rock sculptures found elsewhere in Fars, record triumphant episodes in the lives of the early kings – Ardeshir I, Shapur I, Bahram II and Hormuz II.

Before identification through nineteenth-century research and decipherment of the inscriptions, the sculptures were popularly believed by the Persians to represent episodes in the life of their national hero, Rustam; hence the name Naqsh-e-Rustam, or Pictures of Rustam.

Plate 5 shows the triumph of Shapur I (AD 241–72). The defeated Roman Emperors, Philip the Arab (244–49) and Valerian I (253–60), offer their submission – Philip on bended knee, Valerian with raised arms which are held by Shapur, who had taken him prisoner after the battle of Edessa in 260. Similar scenes are recorded on the rock reliefs at Darab (Plate II) and Shapur.

Plate 6 records the investiture of Ardeshir I (AD 224–41), who overthrew the Parthians and founded the Sassanian dynasty, by the Zoroastrian God, Ahura Mazda, the Lord of Good. Their horses are trampling on their two arch-enemies, Ahriman, the Lord of Evil, and Artabanus V, the last of the Parthian kings.

7 NAQSH-E-RUSTAM, FIRE ALTARS

This pair of altars, in whose hollowed-out tops the holy fire was kindled, are cut from the living rock round the corner of the cliff containing the tombs of four Achaemenian kings – Darius I, Xerxes I, Artaxerxes I and Darius II. The larger is 5 ft. 10 in. high, the other 8 in. shorter. They command a fine view over the Marvdasht plain. Despite a school of thought that attributes an Achaemenian origin to these altars, the weight of opinion today is that they are Sassanian and, as such, constitute the most handsome open-air altars known from that time. Fire worship had already played an important role in Achaemenian times and it remained a vital element in the still later Zoroastrian faith of the Sassanians.

8–13 PERSEPOLIS

Persepolis, 40 miles north-east of Shiraz by road, was the religious and ceremonial capital of the Achaemenian kings from the time of Darius I (521–485 BC) until its destruction by fire when occupied by Alexander the Great in 331 BC.

The various royal buildings – palaces, audience halls, treasury, store rooms, stables, etc. – were built, according to archaeological evidence, by Darius and his successors, Xerxes I (485–465 BC) and Artaxerxes I (465–424), to a plan designed for the 33-acre site as a whole, which was surrounded by a mud-brick wall. They stand on an enormous artificial platform faced with massive blocks of stone and are set against the Kuh-e-Rahmat (Mountain of Mercy) with the Marvdasht plain below. The platform is reached by a great double flight of stone steps, so wide and beautifully proportioned that groups of horsemen could mount them. Most of the brickwork and all the timber columns and roofing have long since disappeared, but stonework has survived, much of it with cuneiform inscriptions or sculpture, cut in low relief, which decorated walls, windows and stairways, and are the chief wonders of Persepolis.

In winter the Achaemenian kings resided at Susa and in summer at Ecbatana, the modern Hamadan, which were the Empire's two administrative capitals. They visited Persepolis each spring for the New Year festival there, the greatest holiday of the Achaemenian religious cycle. The Persian New Year, or *Nau Ruz,* still begins at the Spring Equinox and remains the greatest holiday of the year; also, many of the rites which accompany it, such as jumping over fire and water, are survivals from Achaemenian times.

8 TWO SECTIONS OF A COLUMN CAPITAL
The fluted stone columns, 60 ft. or more tall, which supported the roofs of the various palaces and halls at Persepolis, were crowned with some of the most elaborate capitals ever devised. Here we see two typical elements – a corolla-like capital rising from a wreath of leaves turned down like sepals and a higher piece composed of eight vertical double scrolls – each of which once supported yet another broader stone with the opposed foreparts of either bulls, bull-men or griffins.

9 DOORWAY OF THE TACHARA, OR WINTER PALACE
Bas-relief showing a struggle between the king and a fabulous monster.

Cuneiform inscriptions in the two door-jambs identify the building as the Tachara, or Winter Palace. Other inscriptions record that it was begun by Darius and completed by his son Xerxes. Unlike the other Persepolis palaces, the windows face south over the Marvdasht plain to catch the winter sun.

10 APADANA STAIRWAY
The Apadana, or great Audience Hall, of Darius I, the outstanding building of

Persepolis, stands on a platform approached by staircases to the north and east, which are decorated by bas-reliefs of the highest quality. They depict Persian nobles and officials chattering informally, on their way to attend the King's New Year reception. Below are stylized palm trees.

11, 12 APADANA, EASTERN STAIRCASE

Thanks to having been buried, perhaps at the time of Alexander's destruction, under sand and rubble for some 2,000 years, the bas-reliefs on this staircase are in almost perfect condition and provide a unique illustration of the quality of Achaemenian workmanship and of the diversity of the Empire's subject races. Here in three registers are twenty-three scenes, set between stylized cypress trees, of representatives from various vassal countries (each led by an usher, either Median with low round hat, or Persian with tall hat) come to offer gifts to their sovereign on the occasion of his New Year's reception. Plate 11 shows Babylonians bringing vessels of gold and silver, cloth, and a humped bull, and (below) Syrians with vases, bowls, bracelets, and a chariot drawn by two horses. Plate 12 shows Scythians bringing a horse, bracelets, cloak, and trousers, and (below) Lydians from Sardis with precious bowls and woven stuffs. Elsewhere are depicted Ethiopians, Libyans, Egyptians and Indians. Originally these bas-reliefs were coloured and the metal trappings gilded.

13 APADANA, NORTHERN STAIRCASE

Some idea of the size of the Apadana can be gained from this impressive staircase and the number of columns still standing on the platform to which it leads. The central hall measured 195 ft. square; its wooden roof was supported by six rows of six 61-ft.-high fluted stone columns, with capitals of complex design crowned by double-headed bulls. Two rows of six columns ran round three sides of the hall, entered by two principal doors of wood studded with bronze and gold. Polychrome glazed tiles formed an effective frieze high on the building's exterior.

14 BISITUN, THE MONUMENT OF DARIUS

Darius's famous trilingual monument is cut in the rock face of a cliff 225 ft. above the main Baghdad–Tehran road, 25 miles east of Kermanshah. Begun in 521 BC and probably finished three years later, it consists, in addition to the cuneiform inscriptions, of a bas-relief 18 ft. long showing a 6 ft. tall Darius facing nine rebels from different parts of his empire. The last of these figures, who are roped together, wears a pointed Scythian hat, and was added after the completion of the Elamite inscription which, as can be seen in the photograph, had to be partly obliterated to make room for it. Darius has his left foot on his arch-enemy Gaumata; behind him stand his bow and lance bearers; above the prisoners is the winged figure of the Great King's God, Ahura Mazda. The four columns of inscription in Old Persian below the bas-relief tell of Darius's achievements. Inscriptions in Babylonian and Elamite (the two other principal languages of the Achaemenian Empire) to the left and right of the Old Persian repeat the story and give the line of his descent from Achaemenes, the eponymous founder of the Achaemenian dynasty.

It was a 25-year-old British officer, Major H. C. Rawlinson (later, 1859–60, as Sir Henry Rawlinson, British Minister to Persia) who, while stationed in Kermanshah helping to reorganize the Persian army, began in 1835 the laborious and hazardous task of copying the inscriptions which, when completed in 1846 with the publication of his texts and translations, provided the key to the decipherment of Old Persian and other cuneiform scripts. Over a hundred years later, in 1948, Professor George Cameron of the University of Michigan succeeded in taking latex rubber impressions of the inscriptions, including some which had been inaccessible to Rawlinson.

15 TAQ-E-BUSTAN, SASSANIAN BAS-RELIEF OF STAG HUNT

The bas-reliefs at Taq-e-Bustan (Arch of the Garden), four miles north-east of Kermanshah, are, with one exception, the only Sassanian rock carvings outside Fars; they are also the latest of the Sassanian carvings.

The bas-reliefs decorate two grottoes which have been cut out of a rock cliff rising high above a pool of clear water, which recalls the Sassanian site at Darab (Plate II). The smaller grotto dates from the late fourth century; the larger, which incorporates the stag hunt illustrated here, from the reign of Khosrow II (590–628), who is himself shown at the back of the grotto being invested as king. The stag and boar hunting scenes on the grotto's side walls are unique in that their style is that of Sassanian palace murals. In the stag-hunt scenes beaters are mounted on elephants; the mounted king is seen under an umbrella, while female musicians play on a platform to his right; other scenes show him in full cry after the stag and, finally, when the hunt is over.

16 CTESIPHON, TAQ-E-KISRA (KHOSROW'S ARCH)

Despite an Arab tradition which credits Khosrow I with the building of the great Sassanian Palace at Ctesiphon, it is now generally accepted that it was Shapur I, in the middle of the 3rd century, who made Ctesiphon the capital of the Sassanian Empire and built the palace there.

Little except that shown in the photograph now survives of what was the most extensive of royal Sassanian residences. The brick vault, over 82 ft. wide and 110 ft. high, covered the Throne Room, 160 ft. deep, where the Sassanian kings gave audience in a lavish setting of silks, brocades and jewels. This huge *ivan* was flanked on each side by a six-storeyed brick façade, decorated with blind arches and engaged columns, behind which lay the other palace rooms. The southern wing of the façade is all that now stands, the northern wing having been washed away by floods in 1909.

Ctesiphon is in Iraq on the left bank of the Tigris, 20 miles south-east of Baghdad, opposite the ruins of the Hellenistic city of Seleucia, and was an important Parthian city before becoming the Sassanian capital. It was captured by the Arabs in 637, after which its fortunes declined.

17 SUSA, THE ELAMITE TOWN

Although an Englishman, W. K. Loftus, was the first archaeologist, in 1852, un-questionably to identify the modern Shush with the classical Susa and the Biblical Shushan, it is to a succession of French archaeologists, Dieulafoy, de Morgan, de Mecquenem, Ghirshman and Perrot, that credit is due for the systematic excavation of the site. Since 1897, when the French were granted a monopoly (restricted in 1928) of archaeological excavation in Persia, they have maintained a permanent archaeological mission in Persia and concentrated their main effort on the four great mounds of Susa which dominate the Khuzistan plain between the Karka and Dez Rivers, about 65 miles north of Ahwaz.

Pottery dating back to the 4th millennium BC proves that Susa was one of the oldest cities in the world. It was the Elamite capital from at least the end of the 3rd millennium down to 640 BC, when it was sacked by the Assyrians. Cyrus the Great probably hastened the revival of the city, which became the winter capital of the Achaemenians, while Darius I and Ataxerxes Mnemon built great palaces there. Alexander the Great captured it in 331 BC. Destroyed and rebuilt by the Sassanians, it prospered under them and the Arabs, but steadily declined after the Mongol invasion of Persia.

The Elamite houses shown here date from the early 2nd millennium BC and are situated at the heart of the royal town immediately to the west of the acropolis, below fourteen later habitation levels.

18 HAFT TEPEH, ELAMITE REMAINS

Haft Tepeh (Seven Mounds) is in Khuzistan province about half-way between Andi-meshk and Ahwaz. In 1966 Dr Ezzatullah Neghaban, Director of the Iranian Ar-chaeological Museum, began excavations of the Elamite town of Tikni there, uncovering extensive mud-brick buildings, domestic and religious, of the middle Elamite period (2nd millennium BC).

The view in the photograph looks from the recent south-easterly extension of the excavations towards the slight rise of the main temple and tombs.

The transmission lines by the side of the excavations carry electric power from the huge Dez Dam, north of Andimeshk. Stored water from this dam has been largely responsible for the revival, near Haft Tepeh, of sugar cane cultivation, which flourished in this part of Persia during the Middle Ages. Sugar cane is now grown on about 10,000 acres, and the nearby sugar mill already produces some 45,000 tons of sugar a year.

19 SARVISTAN, SASSANIAN PALACE

Situated in open country 6 miles south of the village of Sarvistan in eastern Fars, this ruined palace is now generally accepted as dating from the reign of Bahram V (AD 420–38). It was built of stone and mortar; behind its eastern façade of three *ivans*, or porches, there was a square domed hall with residential rooms grouped around a central courtyard beyond.

This unadorned ruin has less appeal for the average tourist than for the architectural student interested in the development of Sassanian architecture in the 200 years since Ardeshir I built his palace at Firuzabad. The vaulting is particularly interesting. While Pope regards the columns used as supports for the vaulting in the side rooms as an important constructional innovation, Godard is convinced that they and the semi-domes they supported had only a decorative function.

20 TCHOGA ZANBIL, THE ZIGGURAT OF DUR-UNTASH
FROM THE SOUTH-EAST

Ziggurats, or pyramidal towers of three to seven storeys, usually crowned by a sanctuary, were the religious temples of ancient Mesopotamia, and have been found in all the larger Sumerian, Babylonian and Assyrian cities. In the neighbouring kingdom of Elam (in what is today the south-western Persian province of Khuzistan), King Untash-Gal, in about 1250 BC, built a walled town named Dur-Untash on the right bank of the River Dez about 30 miles south-east of his capital at Susa (Plate 17). A great Ziggurat enclosed within walls about a quarter of a mile square was erected in the centre of the town. In 640 BC the Assyrian King, Assur-Banipal, destroyed Dur-Untash, which was then lost to history until, in 1935, two British geologists prospecting on behalf of the Anglo-Persian Oil Company (now The British Petroleum Co. Ltd) found at Tchoga Zanbil, as the place is now known, a brick inscribed in cuneiform writing, which enabled de Mecquenem, the head of the French Archaeological Mission at Susa, to identify the site.

Dur-Untash was systematically excavated between 1951 and 1962 by Dr Roman Ghirshman, then head of the French Archaeological Mission. The excavations disclosed the largest (346 ft. square, 174 ft. high) and best-preserved Ziggurat yet found.

It was built of sun-dried brick, faced with fired brick, and consisted of five storeys (of which only two had survived) which were once surmounted by a sanctuary. Each of the five storeys had been built up from the ground and not superimposed one on the other.

On this south-east side of the Ziggurat, Ghirshman discovered two temples dedicated to Inshushinak, the principal Elamite god, which he believes were used as places of worship while the main building was being completed.

21 Susa, Palace of Darius

Very little remains today of the great palace Darius I began building in 517 BC on a large artificial platform in the north-west section of the old Elamite city. A clay tablet found there describes how men and material were imported from all over the Achaemenian Empire to help with the building.

The palace, with its magnificent polychrome glazed brick friezes of archers, lions and bulls, now in the Louvre, was discovered by Loftus in 1852 and excavated by Dieulafoy in 1884.

22 Tchoga Zanbil, south-west entrance to the Ziggurat

In the centre of each of the Ziggurat's four sides there were monumental vaulted doorways, identical in design, and baked brick steps leading to the first terrace. The four upper terraces, probably reserved for the priesthood, could only be reached by the south-west stairway shown here.

The circular brick podium at the foot of the stairs still defies interpretation. Its inscribed bricks state that it was dedicated to the gods Gal and Inshushinak.

23 Masjid-e-Sang (Stone Mosque) near Darab

Darab is a small agricultural town about 170 miles south-east of Shiraz near the site of the old Sassanian town of Darabgerd. A low limestone ridge on its southern outskirts contains two interesting monuments cut from the rock, one being the so-called 'Stone Mosque' and the other, about 3 miles away, a great Sassanian bas-relief (Plate II).

The illustration shows the artificially smoothed rock façade and entrance to the rock chamber which may originally have been an early Christian church since it has what could be an altar niche at its east end and a nave and transepts, with aisle running round them, cut from the living rock, as in the famous Ethiopian rock churches at Lalibella. It is also known that Darabgerd was a seat of a Nestorian bishop in Sassanian times. A rock-cut inscription in Arabic dated 1254 and another quoting from the Koran indicate that at one time the chamber served as a mosque. Remnants of plaster remain on the walls, and lighting is provided by a skylight cut through the rock above.

The arched opening to the right leads to a separate and smaller chamber, possibly once a hermit's cell. The water conduit in the foreground has been carefully cut out of the living rock and leads to the ruined town of Jarrat Shahr. Its date is unknown, though undoubtedly it is of considerable antiquity.

Part Two　　FARS AND THE EASTERN DESERT AREA

31

32

33

34

35

36

38

39

40

41

42

43

48

51

54

55

57

58

59

60

24 ISFAHAN, DOME AND MINARETS OF THE THEOLOGICAL COLLEGE
OF THE MOTHER OF THE SHAH (MADRESSEH-E-MADER-E-SHAH)

The American scholar, Arthur Upham Pope, whose monumental *A Survey of Persian Art* in six volumes is indispensable to all students of that subject, describes this Madresseh as 'perhaps the last great building in Iran'. It was built between 1706 and 1714 during the reign of Shah Sultan Hussein, the last of the Safavids. The Shah's mother is said to have paid for the building and also for that of the adjoining caravanserai which was to provide the College's endowment and which was converted in 1962–65 into what is perhaps the most surprising and luxurious hotel in the Middle East.

The great tiled dome over the sanctuary at the north end of the building is covered with large arabesques in yellow, black and white against a brilliant turquoise background. Round the drum runs a band of contrasting lapis lazuli blue decorated with white calligraphic inscriptions. The brilliance of colouring of the dome and minarets is emphasized by the khaki-coloured brickwork below.

Lord Curzon, statesman and traveller, whose *Persia and the Persian Question*, published in 1892, is a mine of invaluable information, described the Madresseh as 'one of the stateliest ruins that I saw in Persia'. It has recently been skilfully restored and is still used as a mosque, though no longer as a seminary. (See also Plate IV.)

25 ISFAHAN, ROYAL MOSQUE (MASJID-E-SHAH)

This aerial photograph shows the Royal Mosque's great central court, with its four *ivans* set between two-storeyed arcades. The south-west *ivan* between two minarets opposite the recessed entrance portal leads to the sanctuary chamber under a great turquoise-blue dome, one of the principal landmarks of Isfahan. On each side of the sanctuary are domed oratories leading to smaller single-storey, tiled and arcaded courts, of which one can be seen here.

The single-storey private houses to the left of the mosque are typical examples of 19th-century Persian domestic architecture. The rooms are grouped round a central courtyard in which there is almost invariably a pool of water and on one side the traditional *talar*, or columned porch.

(MASJID-E-SHAH)

The entire wall space of this great court, above a dado of Yazd marble, is covered with dazzling tiles in which blue predominates. Perhaps because of the enormous area involved, a new technique of *haft rangi* (seven colours) tiling, in which a number of colours were combined on one tile in a single firing, was used instead of the slower and more expensive single colour mosaic faience of earlier buildings, where pieces of single-colour tiling were cut and individually fitted according to the overall design. *Haft rangi* tiling has rather less precision and brilliance than mosaic work. Both techniques were used side by side on the mosque's entrance portal. (See also Plate 25.)

27 ISFAHAN, DOME OF THE SHEIKH LUTFULLAH MOSQUE
(MASJID-E-LUTFULLAH)

This exquisite building, more private oratory than public mosque, was erected by Shah Abbas I between 1603 and 1618 on the Royal Maidan facing the Ali Qapu Palace. It is named after the Shah's father-in-law who was a respected divine. There are a number of unusual features about the building: its squat and partly unglazed dome; the absence of a central court and *ivans*; the single sunken sanctuary chamber covered from top to bottom in mosaic faience of the highest quality.

The 42 ft. wide dome rests on a drum pierced by 16 small windows, through whose double grilles the light plays. The tilework of the ceiling is perhaps the most intricate in Isfahan and has the quality of a finely woven carpet.

The building was extensively and skilfully restored between 1954 and 1956.

28 ISFAHAN, THE QAISARIYEH, OR ROYAL BAZAAR

Virtually no Persian town is without its bazaar, usually covered, built of brick and consisting in greater or lesser degree of long, narrow, intersecting lanes, in which crafts-men, retailers and wholesalers, grouped according to their business, work, sell or buy. The bigger bazaars usually include spacious courtyards and warehouses, as well as their own mosques and baths.

Although the tendency today is for enterprising shopkeepers and merchants to move out of the bazaars into the more modern commercial districts which are now developing in most towns, bazaars still play an important role in Persian commercial life.

The Isfahan bazaar, built during the reign of Shah Abbas I, has an impressive, decorated entrance portal on the north side of the Royal Maidan, and is one of the biggest and most lively bazaars anywhere in the Middle East. Within it can be seen the craftsmen for which Isfahan is famous – silversmiths and coppersmiths, printers of textiles and painters of miniatures, quilt-makers and cobblers, potters and carpenters.

29 ISFAHAN, THE ROYAL MAIDAN. DECORATIVE BRASS WORK

Isfahan, with its splendid Safavid buildings, is the main tourist attraction in Persia. Thanks to the rapid development of tourism in recent years the traditional skills of Isfahan's craftsmen, nourished and encouraged by the Government-run *Honarestan*, or School of Arts and Crafts, have received a new lease of life; so, too, has the great Royal Maidan, now alive with shops doing a thriving business selling local products to visitors.

The metal workers of Isfahan are justly renowned. The two outsize brass incense burners here on sale have clearly been made for the American and European tourist trade; they are an example of pierced or fretwork technique, while the teapot and tray display the techniques of hand-embossing and metal engraving respectively.

The four ladies, or rather schoolgirls, in the foreground are wearing the typically Persian *chador* (literally a tent). Both the veil and *chador* were forbidden by Reza Shah; the former is very rarely seen these days, but the *chador* which loosely covers the body from head to foot is still much worn out of doors by women and girls, except tribal women. It is, however, gradually disappearing under the impact of westernization.

30 ISFAHAN, COFFEE HOUSE (KAHVEH KHANEH)

The coffee house is as Persian an institution as the pub is an English one. It is, however, curiously misnamed, for the Persians, like their Russian and Afghan neighbours but unlike their other neighbours, the coffee-drinking Turks and Arabs, are tea drinkers. Persians sip their tea, weak and well sweetened, from small glasses, called by the Russian name of *istekan*.

Benches, rather than chairs, are the usual furniture of the Persian coffee house. They are covered with bright rugs, and *qilims*, on which customers squat, while at night they are used as beds. The rugs in this photograph can be recognized by their traditional designs as having been woven by women and children of the great Bakhtiari tribe.

31 ISFAHAN, COURT OF THE FRIDAY MOSQUE (MASJID-E-JUMEH)

Described by Pope as 'one of the greatest mosques in the world', more than 800 years of architecture from the 11th to 18th century are displayed in this building. The four-*ivan* court measures 196 by 230 ft.; its mosaic tiling (recently restored) probably dates from the 15th century. The mosque's chief glories, however, are its two late 11th-century Seljuk domes, and its Mongol stucco *mihrab* (see Plate 32).

The larger dome can be seen peeping over the sanctuary *ivan* between the two 15th-century minarets. It was built by Malek Shah's famous vizier, Nizam-ul-Mulk, and is supported by twelve massive piers. The smaller dome, built by the Nizam's rival and successor in 1088 at the northern end of the courtyard, rests on a succession of arches, large and small, ending in sixteen little arches below the dome itself. For Robert Byron this small dome chamber was the 'perfection of architecture' and for Eric Schroeder 'the most beautiful structure in Persia'. Both dome chambers contain some of the finest Seljuk brickwork to be found in Persia.

The cage-like structure on top of the *ivan* is known as a *gul dasteh* (bunch of flowers), as too are the balconies of the minarets. It is from these that the call to prayer is made, nowadays usually by loudspeaker.

32 ISFAHAN, FRIDAY MOSQUE. OLJEITU MIHRAB

Devout Moslems are expected to pray five times daily in the direction of Mecca. When they do so in mosques they face the *qibla* wall which, like churches which face Jerusalem, should be aligned towards Islam's holiest city. The most sacred point in the *qibla* wall is the *mihrab*, usually an arched and decorated niche of stucco or faience tile; near it may stand a *mimbar*, or pulpit, of stone or wood, often beautifully carved.

The Oljeitu Mihrab, named after the Mongol Ilkhan, who ruled Persia between 1304 and 1316 and caused the Friday Mosque to be embellished, is of chiselled stucco and dated 1310. It is, in Pope's view, 'the most subtle and perfectly proportioned of the 14th-century *mihrabs*'. The intricate design of leaves, tendrils and blossoms is framed within inscriptions beautifully executed in the Nakshi and Kufic style under an over-panel of lotuses. On each side are two carved *mimbars* probably dating from the Safavid period.

33 ISFAHAN, FRIDAY MOSQUE. STALACTITE DECORATION

Detail of stalactite decoration, probably 18th-century, in the west *ivan* showing light and dark blue faience cubes set in buff brickwork.

Note also the faience inscription in cursive Nakshi script running beneath the stalactites. The Persians have throughout the centuries made much use of the decorative qualities of the Arabian script in their mosques, usually to quote phrases from the Koran.

34 CARAVANSERAI AT MAHYAR

Mahyar is 30 miles south of Isfahan on the main road to Shiraz; this 17th-century caravanserai of brick on a stone foundation was, according to Curzon, originally built by the mother of Shah Abbas and later restored by Shah Suleiman. At the beginning of the 19th century it was said to be 'the finest erection of the kind in Persia', but it was in a state of dilapidation by the time Curzon saw it in 1889.

Caravanserais were the motels of the pre-motor age. They provided shelter and protection, as well as water and sometimes food, for the traveller and his animals. Ruined caravanserais dating from the early 12th to the late 19th century can still be seen strung out along many of the old caravan routes of Persia, usually a day's march or about 20 miles apart. Their basic design, on the Persian mosque plan of a central court with arcaded sides and four *ivans*, remained more or less unchanged throughout the centuries. For security reasons there would usually be only one entrance, often, as here, with a second storey over the arch where important travellers were lodged, and useful for defence in case of need. Vaulted recesses raised 2 to 5 ft. from the ground, with a small room behind, provided privacy and accommodation for travellers, who would cook their own meals there. Animals were stabled in the passage between these rooms and the outer wall, baggage and merchandise being stacked in the central courtyard. Sometimes, as shown here, the outer walls contained vaulted recesses where travellers could rest, sleep and tether their animals so long as there was no danger of attack by raiders. The bigger caravanserais often had their own baths and oratories. (See also Plates 45 and 60.)

35 ISFAHAN, FRIDAY MOSQUE. ROOFING BEHIND THE WEST IVAN
The perforated domes provide ventilation for the mosque's ancient lavatories and toilets immediately below. Beyond can be seen the flat roof of the enclosed and vaulted Winter Prayer Hall, built in 1447 and ingeniously illuminated by translucent alabaster slabs let into the roofing.

36 PIGEON TOWERS AND STORKS NEAR ISFAHAN
A curiosity of the countryside around Isfahan, first noted by the Moorish traveller, Ibn Battuta, who visited Isfahan about 1330, and remarked on by European travellers from the 17th century onwards, are the pigeon towers, like fortresses or great chessmen, dotted among fields and gardens. Of the 3,000 once said to exist, many have disappeared or are in ruins; relatively few remain in use today. Their purpose, however, is still to collect pigeon manure, long considered by Isfahanis the best fertilizer for their famous melon fields. To this end the towers are ingeniously designed to provide the maximum number of holes and perches for the pigeons, who enter and leave the towers through the honey-comb brickwork 'pepper pot' tops, the manure being collected once a year. The bigger towers house up to 10,000 birds.

No two towers are quite alike, individual designs being handed down within each family or village. The bigger towers are free-standing; others are built into walls of houses or gardens. Built of sun-dried brick, usually without timber, they were originally covered with white plaster and often adorned with polychrome cupolas and friezes.

37 NEW JULFA (ISFAHAN), DOMED CEILING AND NORTH TRANSEPT ARCH OF ALL SAVIOURS' CATHEDRAL
Following his successful campaigns in Armenia and Georgia in the early years of the 17th century, Shah Abbas I forcibly transplanted thousands of Armenian and Georgian

families. The Armenians from Julfa on the River Araxes (which since 1828 has been the north-west frontier between Persia and the USSR) were settled by the south bank of the Zaindeh Rud on the outskirts of Isfahan. Shah Abbas's purposes in doing this were varied; certainly one of them was to make use of Armenian skill, thrift and industry to develop the commercial life of his new capital.

The Armenians called their new home after their old one and were allowed to build churches and to practise their Christianity, which they do to this day. Thirteen churches built between 1606 and 1728 still survive, though the number of Armenians has now dwindled to about 5,000 souls.

All Saviours' Cathedral (popularly known as the Vank) was probably begun in 1606 and largely rebuilt between 1655 and 1664. Its design is very much that of the domed sanctuary chamber of a Persian mosque, with the addition of a raised chancel and altar within a semi-octagonal apse. By contrast to its modest exterior, the cathedral's interior is lavishly decorated. The floor is richly carpeted: above a wainscoting of bright yellow and blue tiles dating from the early 18th century the walls are covered with murals, oil paintings and gilded stucco. The ceiling of the dome and the four large supporting arches are painted in blue and gold.

38 ISFAHAN, SHAHRESTAN BRIDGE FROM THE SOUTH

The Shahrestan is the oldest and furthest downstream of Isfahan's five bridges across the Zaindeh Rud (Life-Giving River), which rises in the Bakhtiari mountains and eventually loses itself in the desert to the east of Isfahan. The bridge, which is little used these days, is slightly hump-backed. The stone piers and prow-like blocks of stone on which they stand are thought to be Sassanian, and the brickwork above early Islamic, probably Seljuk. The main and secondary arches which pierce the brickwork are linked by side vents designed to allow the maximum flow of water at flood time. This, as Pope states, is a peculiarly Roman device introduced to Persia by Roman prisoners, captured at the battle of Edessa in AD 260, who helped to build the bridges at Shushtar and Dezful.

The ruined building at the north end of the bridge was probably a toll house.

39 ISFAHAN, ALLAH VERDI KHAN BRIDGE

The Allah Verdi Khan bridge, known locally as the 'Si-o-seh pul' (Bridge of Thirty-Three Arches), was built about 1602 by Shah Abbas I's favourite General, Allah Verdi Khan. Curzon thought it probably 'the stateliest bridge in the world'. It consists of a two-storeyed succession of arches, brick on stone piers, and is 968 ft. long by 45 ft. wide. Its main roadway is flanked by covered arcades where pedestrians can stroll at ease or picnic in the niches overlooking the river. Stairs lead to promenades, both below and above the road level, which run the full length of the bridge – below, through a covered arcade, and above, along the bridge's parapet.

The bridge was built to link Shah Abbas's famous Chahar Bagh (Four Gardens), still Isfahan's main thoroughfare, with the royal gardens at Hazar Jarib and the nearby Armenian settlement created by Shah Abbas at Julfa, on the southern bank of the river.

40 ISFAHAN, KHWAJU BRIDGE

This magnificent bridge, 429 by 39 ft., named after the district it serves, was built in the reign of Shah Abbas II (1642–67) and in Pope's view is 'the culminating monument of Persian bridge architecture'. With its two-storeyed succession of 23 arches of brick on massive stone piers, and its roadway running between high walls arcaded on the outer side, the bridge is closely related in design to the nearby Allah Verdi Khan Bridge, built some fifty years earlier (Plate 39). Its lines are, however, more pleasing, due in part to the attractive pavilions in the centre and at either end of the bridge.

The bridge was also built to serve as a dam, the stone piers on the upstream side being pierced by narrow channels which can be blocked by sluice gates, thus enabling the water level to be controlled, both for irrigation purposes and to form a decorative lake in front of the big houses which lined the bank in Safavid days. On the downstream side great flights of stone steps lead to the water: it is here that generations of Isfahanis have picnicked and done their washing.

41 SHIRAZ, TOMB OF HAFEZ

It comes as a surprise to many westerners brought up on Edward Fitzgerald's translation of Omar Khayyam to learn that for most Persians the greatest of their poets is Shams-ud-Din Muhammed, better known as Hafez, *i.e.* one who has learned the Koran by heart.

Hafez was born in Shiraz in 1324, chose to live there all his life, sang its praises in incomparable verse and was buried there in 1389 in a garden known after him as the Hafezieh, in the north-east part of the city. The present mausoleum and garden date from 1936–38. They are approached by flights of stone steps, at the top of which a double colonnade is crossed to reach the tomb under a tiled cupola. The alabaster tombstone and four central columns of the colonnade alone date from the reign of Karim Khan Zand. The tombstone is beautifully inscribed with two of Hafez's *ghazals*. Visitors to the tomb can still, as they have done for centuries, take the omens, or *fal*, by picking a page at random from a volume of Hafez, kept ready for this purpose.

The mysticism and symbolism of much of Hafez's verse makes translation difficult. Miss Gertrude Bell is generally considered his most successful English translator. At the age of 23, before becoming absorbed in the Arab world, she had spent much of the year 1892 at the British Legation in Tehran studying the Persian language and literature. Her *Poems from the Divan of Hafez* was published in 1897.

Sa'di (*c.* 1209–91) was born and died in Shiraz. Like his fellow Shirazi, Hafez, he is one of the great names in Persian literature. He was educated in Baghdad and then travelled in the Middle East, North Africa and India before settling in Shiraz where, drawing on his wide experiences, he set down in verse and prose his eminently sensible views on life and human nature. His best known works are the *Gulestan* (The Rose Garden) and the *Bustan* (The Orchard). Like Shakespeare, Sa'di is always being quoted and is popularly referred to by Persians as 'the Shaikh'.

Sa'di is buried near Hafez. So that their last resting places should be worthy of them, the Persian authorities have in recent years completely rebuilt their tombs. Sa'di's was completed in 1952. Though modern in its simplicity, the portico or *talar* with its tall columns of pinkish marble is a traditional feature of Persian architecture. Steps lead up to the tomb with its turquoise-blue dome. A short double colonnade to the left leads to a tiled sunken enclosure containing a pool filled with voracious fish.

43 SHIRAZ, THE KHODA KHANEH OF THE FRIDAY MOSQUE

The Friday Mosque is Shiraz's oldest mosque, though very little of the original 9th-century building remains, apart from some stonework and a section of the stucco *mihrab*.

A curious feature, found in no other Persian mosque, is the structure known as the Khoda Khaneh (God's House) in the centre of the main court, used as a depository for the mosque's Korans. It was built in 1351 in imitation of the *Kaaba* at Mecca, round which pilgrims are bound as a religious act to circumambulate seven times. No such performance is demanded in Shiraz.

The Khoda Khaneh, a nearly square building faced with stone, was in a ruinous state for many years but was restored between 1937 and 1954. A unique feature is the beautiful inscriptive frieze in stone relief set within blue mosaic faience.

44 SHIRAZ, WINTER PRAYER HALL OF THE MOSQUE OF THE REGENT (MASJID-E-VAKIL)

As its name implies, this mosque was built by Karim Khan Zand, the Vakil or Regent of Persia, who made Shiraz his capital and did much to beautify it between 1750 and 1779. The mosque, which adjoins the bazaar also built by the Vakil, was completed in 1773 and restored in 1825. It has only two *ivans* instead of the usual four, on the northern and southern sides of a large open court. The *ivans* and court are decorated with typical Shirazi *haft rangi* tiles. Their gay colours and floral designs attracted the admiration of Pierre Loti and give a special charm to this unusual building.

The large winter prayer hall behind the south *ivan* is supported by a veritable forest of 44 monolithic pillars carved in spirals, each with a capital of acanthus leaves. The *mimbar*, or pulpit, in this hall is cut from a solid piece of marble.

45 KERMAN, CARAVANSERAI-E-VAKIL

Built by Mohammed Ismail Khan, Vakil-ul-Mulk, who was an energetic Governor
of Kerman from 1859 to 1866, this caravanserai, with its attractively tiled walls, adjoins
the main Vakil Bazaar, whose 600-yards main avenue is the longest of any bazaar in
Persia. The caravanserai provides office accommodation and storage room for bazaar
merchants. The two handsome 'chimneys' are in fact *badgirs* (wind towers), which are
a common feature of Kerman, Yazd and other desert towns. They have open vents in
which slats are set and manipulated to catch such breezes as may be blowing; cool
air is thus drawn down to basement rooms which are used during the scorching summer
months. The summer temperature in these rooms is between 20 and 30 degrees cooler
than in those above ground.

46 KERMAN, ENTRANCE TO THE THEOLOGICAL COLLEGE (MADRESSEH)
AND BATH HOUSE (HAMMAM) OF IBRAHIM KHAN

Perhaps the most enchanting corner of Kerman bazaar is this, where the entrances to
the Madresseh (on right) and *hammam* adjoin. Built in 1816–17 by a cousin and son-in-
law of Fath Ali Shah, Ibrahim Khan, who was Governor of Kerman from 1801 to
1824, the entrance portals are decorated with gay tilework, whose designs include
peacocks, water fowl, flowers and calligraphic inscriptions. The interiors of both
buildings are worthy of their entrances. The tiled and single-storey Madresseh is built
round a peaceful, cypress-shaded courtyard, while the walls of the *hammam* are decorated
with amusing paintings said to date from the end of the 18th century.

47 RUINS OF BAM

Bam, an oasis town on the southern fringe of the Kavir-e-Lut, or Great Sand Desert,
between Kerman and Zahedan, has an ancient history, much of it not recorded. In the
early Middle Ages, Bam was renowned for its palm trees, impregnable castle and cotton
manufactures. Today there are really two Bams side by side – the old frontier post of
Kerman province, now a ghost town totally abandoned within its high crenellated
walls of sun-dried brick; and the new town built in the 1850s in the well-watered plain
below where fruit, especially dates, oranges and grapefruit, are grown, as well as henna.

As a fortified frontier post Bam was often attacked by Afghans, Baluchis and Sistanis.
It fell to Afghan forces in 1719 and again in 1721. In 1795 it was the scene of the final
stand of the last of the Zands, Lutf Ali Khan; and was abandoned in favour of the new
site after withstanding siege by Afghan and Sistan forces in 1850.

The view is from the citadel of the old ruins (probably dating from 17th–19th century).
The well-watered oasis can be seen beyond the walls.

There is no more impressive gateway in Persia than this great soaring 14th-century edifice, here shown from the roof of the mosque with part of the dome in the foreground. Crowned by a pair of minarets, the highest in Persia, the portal's façade is decorated from top to bottom in dazzling tilework, predominantly blue in colour. Within there is a long arcaded court where, behind a deep-set south-east *ivan*, is a sanctuary chamber. This chamber, under a squat tiled dome, is exquisitely decorated with faience mosaic: its tall faience *mihrab*, dated 1365, is one of the finest of its kind in existence.

The mosque was largely rebuilt between 1324 and 1365, and is one of the outstanding 14th-century buildings in Persia. The tilework has recently been skilfully restored and a modern library built to house the mosque's valuable collection of books and manuscripts.

Yazd, a great desert town in the centre of Persia, is the main stronghold of the ancient Zoroastrian community. It was visited in 1272 by Marco Polo, who described it as 'a good and noble city' which manufactured silk. Today it remains a town of high mud-brick walls and narrow passageways, known, however, for its modern textile mills, its marble and henna, and for the honesty and industry of its people.

49 YAZD, TAKIEH-YE-MIR CHAQMAQ

Although described more often than not as an entrance portal to the bazaar, this early 19th-century tiled edifice was built to serve as a grandstand for the traditional passion play, or *Ta'azieh*, recording the martyrdom of the third Imam, Hussein, that used to be acted during the mourning month of *Muharram* in the *Takieh*, or special theatre used for these performances, of which it formed part. It also provided an imposing entrance to one of Yazd's bazaars.

However, both the bazaar and all but this remnant of the *Takieh* have disappeared, so that it is now only a picturesque façade and landmark in the centre of Yazd near the 15th-century Amir Chaqmaq mosque.

The *Ta'azieh*, forbidden during Reza Shah's reign, is still performed in town and village *Takiehs* during the first ten days of the lunar month of *Muharram*.

50 YAZD, OLD TOWN WALLS

Little trace remains today of the old fortified walls of sun-dried brick which used to surround Persian towns. Tehran's walls were demolished by Nasr-ud-din Shah and replaced in the 1870s by a rampart and fosse, pierced by twelve gates, modelled on Vauban's Paris fortifications. These in turn were demolished by Reza Shah, the twelve city gates finally disappearing in 1934. The walls of the ghost city of old Bam (Plate 47) are the most complete that survive, while in Yazd sections of the old walls and moat remain, buried deep within a town which has long since expanded beyond its old limits.

These walls were begun, it is said, in 1119 and rebuilt and extended during the 14th century. In places they were 50 ft. high. What remains provides an interesting example of a medieval wall, fortified by moat, towers and barbicans; in places the wall was nicely decorated with ornamental devices such as those employed on unglazed pottery.

51 YAZD, ZOROASTRIAN TOWER OF SILENCE

Zoroastrianism was the national religion of Sassanian Persia. The estimated 21,000 Zoroastrians in Persia today are descendants of those who, at the time of the Arab conquests, refused to abandon their faith in favour of Islam or to emigrate, as many did, to India, where their descendants are known as Parsees, *i.e.* people from Persia. These Parsees still maintain links with their co-religionists and kinsmen in Persia.

Although about half of today's Zoroastrians live in Tehran, their main strongholds have for centuries been the desert towns of Yazd and Kerman. The Zoroastrians' outward symbol is the cult of fire which is kept burning continuously in their Fire Temples. Although burial in the ground is now more usual, the traditional exposure of the dead within an open enclosure known as a *dakhmeh*, or Tower of Silence, is still sometimes practised at Kerman, Yazd and surrounding Zoroastrian villages. The small building at the foot of the hill illustrated here is an *ateshgah*, or fire altar, where a flame is kept burning from sunset to dawn for three nights after the body has been placed in the tower above.

52 QANAT AND IRRIGATED FIELDS NEAR ISFAHAN

All over the Persian plateau long lines of mounds resembling great molehills converge on towns and villages. These are the visible signs of the 2,500-year-old tunnel-well or *qanat* system first developed in Persia, and still in use there and in other parts of the Middle East and Central Asia, where they were introduced in the wake of the Achaemenian conquests.

A *qanat* is a gently sloped tunnel, sometimes as much as 30 miles long, bringing water by force of gravity from its upland, underground source to the point where it is needed; it is then led into irrigation runnels. Too early surfacing causes loss through evaporation. At intervals of 100 to 300 ft., vertical shafts are dug, both to ventilate the tunnel for the *muqannis* (*qanat* diggers) and to enable the excavated soil to be drawn up in buckets by a hand windlass. These shafts are usually between 100 to 200 ft. deep at the source and diminish in depth as the *qanat* approaches the surface.

Qanat digging is a highly skilled and dangerous operation, handed down from father to son, for which Yazdis are particularly well known. The owner of a *qanat* sells his water on a time basis, *i.e.* so many minutes or hours of flow per day or week.

This mosque, the oldest in use in Persia today, was built about 960 on the Arabian plan of an oblong court surrounded by high arcades. The slightly higher central arch in each side of the court foreshadows the advent of the Persian four-*ivan* plan. The building is noteworthy for its early stucco work, particularly the elaborate decoration of the *mihrab* and surrounding columns and arches in which 'the implicit theme throughout is the age-old concept of fertility . . . entwining vines, closely scrolling stems, dense foliage, colossal blossoms and heavy pendant fruits' (Pope). The stucco calligraphic friezes over the bays and arches are the earliest surviving in Persia. The *mimbar* next to the *mihrab* is a good example of 14th-century wood carving.

Nain lies on the desert road between Kashan and Yazd. The manufacture of the fine woollen *aba*, or cloak, for which Nain was once famous, has now, with the adoption of European dress, given place to carpet weaving. Nain carpets and rugs, which are exceptionally closely woven and elaborate in design, are the finest produced in Persia today, and as such are the gift customarily offered by the Shah or his Ministers to visiting Heads of State and other distinguished guests.

54, 55 ARDISTAN, FRIDAY MOSQUE

Ardistan, 96 miles south-east of Kashan, is a small desert town whose mosque, dating mainly from the 12th century, is one of the earliest examples of the four-*ivan* plan. The building, however, includes traces of 10th-century work and incorporates an 11th-century edifice in the form of what André Godard, Director-General of Antiquities in Persia 1929–59, calls a kiosk mosque, in which the *qibla* wall and *mihrab* were sheltered under a square domed chamber (derived from the Sassanian fire temple), the other three sides of the court being left wide open.

Plate 54 is a detail of the entrance *ivan* showing 12th-century stucco inscriptions decorating the soffits of the arch and the frieze beyond; also imitation brick-bonding, executed by covering brick surface with plaster which was then marked out in interesting brick patterns; patterned brick end-plugs were then inserted.

The mosque's domed sanctuary chamber contains some of the best Seljuk brickwork to be found outside Isfahan, as well as a fine 12th-century stucco *mihrab* and calligraphic frieze dated 1160 running below the dome.

Plate 55 shows the approach to the mosque from the north. Note the absence of all faience tiling.

56 NATANZ, 14TH-CENTURY MINARET

This 123 ft. tall minaret of brick inlaid with monochrome tiles was built in 1324 and is one of four separate but structurally connected buildings, all dating from the

14th century – the others being the Friday Mosque, a tiled tent-domed tomb and the tiled façade of what was once a *Khanagah*, or religious hostelry.

The rounded brick minaret originated in north-east Persia. Persian minarets until the 13th century were almost always erected singly in the north corner of the mosque; thereafter they were usually built in pairs to flank the entrance portal or sanctuary *ivan*. From the 15th century they have usually been decorated with mosaic or *haft rangi* tiles.

Natanz is a picturesque little town 44 miles south-east of Kashan, surrounded by well-watered gardens and mountains, and noted for its pottery. Shah Abbas I had a palace and hunting lodge there.

57 TOMB OF FIRUZ ABU LU LU AT FIN, NEAR KASHAN

Abu Lu Lu was a native of Fin who, when working in Medina, distinguished himself in Shi'ite eyes by allegedly murdering in 664 the second Caliph Omar, whose authority as successor to the Prophet Mohammed is not recognized by Shi'ites. Abu Lu Lu was probably a Zoroastrian, though some claim that he was a Christian.

Abu Lu Lu was himself, according to Persian tradition, killed in Medina. It seems unlikely, therefore, that his body in fact lies beneath the tomb illustrated here and erected in his memory by the Shi'ite inhabitants of Fin in the 15th or 16th century. The building has been repaired and almost completely retiled in recent years.

58 GARDEN OF FIN (BAGH-E-FIN) NEAR KASHAN

This once royal garden of Fin, with its flowers and trees, its spouting water and clear streams running over turquoise tiles, is a superb example of the formal Persian garden. Though favoured by the Safavid kings, the present garden and decorated pavilions date mainly from the reign of Fath Ali Shah (1789–1834). In 1852 Nasr-ud-din Shah's progressive Grand Vizier, Amir Kabir Mirza Taqi Khan, was murdered in the garden's *hammam* by royal command.

The Persian word for paradise, *firdous*, also signifies a garden. Small wonder that gardens and paradise are closely associated in Persian minds when there is such contrast between the arid, treeless nature of so much of the countryside and the cool peace of a high-walled garden, whether *gulestan* (flower garden) or *bustan* (orchard) in which water, running or still, is as important an element as flowers or trees.

59 RUINED YAKH-CHAL NEAR ABARQU

A *yakh-chal* is a place for making and storing ice. Before the age of electricity and refrigerators it was the sole source of ice during the hot Persian summer and was much used in those parts of the country where the winter temperatures could be relied upon to drop below freezing point.

A trench about 2 ft. deep and perhaps 100 yards long would be dug. This would be protected from the sun on the south side by a 20 ft. or higher wall (left of the picture). On the first cold night the trench would be flooded with a few inches of water that would freeze. The same process would be continued on successive nights until the ice was six inches or so thick, when it would be broken up and stored in an adjoining deep pit, protected from the sun by a tall conical roof. Enough ice would, if possible, be produced to fill the pit before the end of winter. Ice stored in this way lasted throughout the summer. Today in remote mountain areas snow is similarly stored for use during the summer.

60 CARAVANSERAI AT SIAHKUH

Siahkuh (Black Mountain) is a desolate spot on the western fringe of the Great Salt Desert about 55 miles south of Varamin. Today, apart from a few game wardens stationed there to protect wild life, particularly ibex, mountain sheep and that rare animal, the *onegar*, or wild ass, there is not a living soul in sight. Yet the ruins of two splendid caravanserais are evidence of the lost importance of Siahkuh, the last staging-post before north-bound travellers faced the hazards of the waterless desert on the ancient caravan track from Kashan to the Caspian.

The Roman traveller Pietro Della Valle stayed at Siahkuh in 1618 on his way from Isfahan to visit Shah Abbas I at Farahabad on the Caspian. By the 19th century Siahkuh was more important for its situation on the route from Isfahan and Kashan to the new capital in Tehran. Today it is all but forgotten.

61 YAZD-E-KHAST

Also spelt Izadkhast, this crumbling village is 80 miles south of Isfahan on the main road to Shiraz and has attracted the attention of generations of travellers and writers. Its main claim to distinction is its curious situation on the top of a great prow-like cliff which itself stands in a deep valley. Because of its precipitous situation Yazd-e-Khast can be entered only at one point on its south-western side over a rather rickety drawbridge.

62 QUM, SHRINE OF FATIMEH THE IMMACULATE (HASRAT-E-MA'SUMEH).
NORTH FAÇADE

The gilded Safavid dome of Fatimeh's tomb chamber stands out clearly here between 19th-century minarets. The squat tiled dome to the left, predominantly blue in colour, was built in the 1950s over what was previously an open court. The big courtyard in the foreground was once a burial ground, whose grave-stones now pave the court.

There is an interesting museum attached to the shrine, as well as a large library, primarily for the use of the many theological students who study in Qum. (See also Plate IX.)

Part Three   AZERBAIJAN, KURDISTAN AND THE WEST

65

66

74

75

76

78

77

79

63 SULTANIYEH, MAUSOLEUM OF OLJEITU KHODABANA BY MOONLIGHT

This view of the 14th-century Oljeitu mausoleum (Plate VIII) near Zanjan is taken from the south-east and shows the great dome, 117 ft. high and 80 ft. in diameter, set, in Pope's words, 'like a diadem' between eight tiled minarets, of which only the stumps now remain. The dome, with a wide Kufic inscription running round its drum, was once covered with turquoise-blue tiles, of which traces remain. The low building on the right is a funerary chapel in which Oljeitu himself is buried. It was probably added to the original octagonal building when Oljeitu had thoughts of developing the main building as a popular pilgrim centre.

64-66 QAZVIN, SHRINE OF SHAH ZADEH HUSSEIN

Shah Zadeh Hussein, the son of the Eighth Imam, was, according to local legend, killed when a roof fell on him after performing a miracle. His shrine has long been an attraction for pilgrims and lies within a spacious courtyard, or rather a cemetery, paved with tomb-stones and surrounded by high, arcaded walls. The elaborately decorated octagonal domed building over his tomb, dating in part from the reign of Shah Tahmasp (1524-76) when Qazvin was the Safavid capital, was erected, according to a tiled inscription, by command of his daughter, Zainab Begum. However, the mirror-work of the *talar* and some of the faience tiling dates from the 19th century.

64 DETAIL OF DECORATIVE MIRROR-WORK

The *talar* of the shrine scintillates with mirror-work such as this. The extensive use of mirror-work as decoration in Persia comes as a surprise to the European visitor; it is, as Pope states, used for architectural ornament 'with a lavishness and boldness that have never been equalled elsewhere. The Hall of Mirrors at Versailles is in itself sufficiently exciting, but conservative compared to the complete interiors composed of mirrors which are not infrequent in Persia.'

The date when decorative mirror-work was first introduced to Persia is unknown; it was certainly popular throughout the 19th century and remains so today. Apart from the decoration of royal palaces and private houses it is much used to adorn shrines, as at Rey, Qum and Meshed.

137

65 ENTRANCE PORTAL

The shrine is approached from the roadway outside through this tiled and domed gateway typical of the 19th-century Qajar period. It is embellished with five minarets and described by Stevens as 'charming if rather decadent'.

66 THE SHRINE

This is the view of Shah Zadeh Hussein's shrine immediately facing the entrance portal. Note the elaborate tile-work, including the inscription above the portico and the dazzling 19th-century mirror-work beyond the columns.

67 TABRIZ, CARPET FACTORY

Persian carpets and rugs have for centuries been made entirely by hand; weaving and knotting is still done on simple traditional looms, usually vertical but also horizontal, by women and children working on looms in their town or village homes. The bigger and finer quality carpets are woven in factories containing a number of looms in which men as well as women and children work. The design, if it is not a traditional one known by heart, is either called out to the weavers by an overseer or placed in front of them, as here. The industry is widespread throughout Persia.

The best Persian carpets are unrivalled in design and quality, the latter being primarily judged by the number of knots to the square inch, which can be as many as 450 in a woollen carpet and up to 800 in one of silk. Tabriz, Meshed, Qum, Kashan, Isfahan, Nain and Kerman are particularly well known for their fine-quality carpets; Hamadan, surrounded by carpet-weaving villages, is the headquarters of the less expensive rug, while tribal rugs, each with their own distinctive designs and colours, are made by the Turkomens and Baluchis in the north-east, by Bakhtiaris in central and western Iran, by the Qashqais, Afshars, etc. in the south, and by the Kurds in the north-west.

Although Persian rugs were known in Europe during the Middle Ages, it was not until the mid-19th century that enterprising Tabrizi merchants started shipping them in commercial quantities *via* Trebizond, a 30-day caravan journey from Tabriz, on the Black Sea to Constantinople (Istanbul), which developed into a great emporium for the European carpet trade. Today carpets are, after oil, Persia's major export.

68 TABRIZ, BLUE MOSQUE (MASJID-E-KABUD). DETAIL OF TILEWORK IN THE MAIN SANCTUARY: NORTH-WEST SIDE

Tabriz (the ancient Tauris), with a population of 405,000, is the capital of East Azer-baijan province and has a long and chequered history. It was an Armenian capital in the third century AD and from 1295 to 1313 the capital of the Mongol Ilkhans; sacked by Tamerlane in 1392, it was the 15th-century capital of the Kara Koyun (Black Sheep)

Turkomens, whose ruler, Shah Jehan, built the famous Blue Mosque in 1465, inspired, it has been suggested, by a determination to assert the Sunni faith in what had long been a Shi'ite stronghold.

The mosque was destroyed by one of Tabriz's recurrent earthquakes and is now a sorry ruin, though sufficient faience tiling remains to give an idea of its former splendour. To achieve this, new techniques and designs were used as well as a new and wider range of colours. Note here the contrast between surfaces wholly decorated with glazed mosaic tiling and the buff brick panel in which brilliant blue medallions decorated in white have been embedded.

69 KURDISH HAMLET SOUTH OF LAKE REZAIYEH

This hamlet at the southern end of Lake Rezaiyeh (formerly Urmia) is typical of the flat-roofed, mud-brick Kurdish villages of the rolling fertile countryside stretching south from the lake; so, too, are the long counterpoised poles for lifting water-buckets from the wells and the pyramids of dried cattle dung used as fuel in an area where timber is scarce.

The origin of the Kurds is obscure, though there is no doubt that, like the Iranians, they belong to the Aryan race and that their language, though distinct from, is related to the Persian language. They have their own national dress and are mostly Sunni Moslems.

Approximately five million Kurds live in the adjacent mountainous regions of north-west Persia, east Turkey and north-east Iraq; the predominantly Kurdish part of Persia roughly stretches from the Turkish and Iraqi borders to the shores of Lake Rezaiyeh and then south-east up to a line running half-way between Sanandaj (formerly Senneh), the capital of Kurdistan province, and Hamadan, bounded on the south by the Hamadan–Kermanshah–Baghdad road. Well over one million Kurds live in Persia today.

70 WEST AZERBAIJAN PROVINCE, CHURCH OF ST THADDEUS,
FROM THE EAST

The black sandstone used for the east or sanctuary end of this ancient Armenian church (Plate VII) accounts for its local Azeri Turkish name of Kara Kilisa (Black Church). Particularly noteworthy are the alternate courses of light and dark stone running round the typically Armenian dome and the bas-reliefs picked out in white stone on the east wall.

The first European traveller to describe the church was Colonel E. J. C. Monteith of the Indian Army in the Journal of the Royal Geographic Society of London in 1832. It was not until 127 years later that another description of the church was published, this time in Armenian by Mr Haik Ajamian. The first detailed study of the site and buildings was made in 1966 by Dr W. Kleiss of the German Archaeological Institute in Tehran.

The church is no longer in use except for an annual service in July, instituted as recently as 1954, on the anniversary of Thaddeus' death. Hundreds of Armenians from Tabriz and the surrounding countryside then make the pilgrimage there, a reminder that the 190,000 Armenians now living in Persia are the country's most numerous and, with the Assyrians, most ancient Christian minority.

71 REZAIYEH BAZAAR

Rezaiyeh has a lively covered bazaar which, though considerably later in date than the Isfahan bazaar (Plate 28), is built upon the same traditional lines. The domed vaults have circular openings to provide light, but they also let in rain and cold so that the tendency today is to cover them with glass. The absence of motor traffic adds greatly to the attraction of these old bazaars.

The man in the foreground with his back to the photographer can only be a Kurd, given his tassled turban and baggy Kurdish trousers.

Previously known as Urmia, or Urmi, Rezaiyeh was renamed after Reza Shah about 1930. According to legend it was the birthplace of Zoroaster and the burial place of one of the Three Magi. Today Rezaiyeh remains the centre of a large and very fertile fruit (mainly grapes) and tobacco-growing plain, inhabited for centuries past by Christian Armenians and Assyrians as well as by Moslem Kurds and Azeri Turks. Of the various European and American Christian Missions who made their head-quarters at Urmia in the 19th century, only the French have survived.

72 REZAIYEH, FRIDAY MOSQUE. DETAILS OF THE MIHRAB

The Friday Mosque, adjoining the bazaar at Rezaiyeh, is an unusual building, dating from Seljuk times, but is thought to incorporate an earlier structure. Like the mosque at Ardistan (Plates 54, 55), it was built on the kiosk plan of a square, domed chamber approached across an open courtyard in which there are none of the customary *ivans* of later mosques. The carved stucco *mihrab*, dated 1277, is richly adorned with the typical decoration of the period – exuberant foliage and geometric patterns framed within panels of beautifully executed Kufic script.

Stucco plaster is known to have been used as a building material in Persia for at least 2,500 years; it was developed as a decorative medium by the Sassanians and continued to be used as such in mosques and shrines, as well as private houses, from early Islamic days until the present.

73 MARAGHEH, THE RED TOMB TOWER (GONBAD-E-SURKH)

Maragheh, 90 miles south of Tabriz, was a town of some importance even before

140

Genghis Khan's grandson Hulagu Khan made it the Mongol capital and built his celebrated observatory there in 1259. Three of Maragheh's four tomb towers (all of them, in Pope's words, 'masterpieces of brick construction') are pre-Mongol, dating from the 12th century. The earliest is the Gonbad-e-Surkh (1147), a square, single-chamber, brick building, once surmounted by an octagonal pyramid roof, of which only the base remains.

Brick has been used to excellent decorative effect on all four sides, while fragments of turquoise-blue faience set into the geometric patterned arch over the north doorway (not visible) was the beginning of what was to become the technique of mosaic faience, which reached its apogee during the 15th century in the Blue Mosque at Tabriz and the Gawhar Shad at Meshed (Plates 68 and 88).

Despite the size of the Maragheh tomb towers and their obvious importance, nothing is known of the identity of those buried in them.

74 KHARRAQAN, SELJUK TOMB TOWERS, FROM THE SOUTH

Situated 75 miles north-east of Hamadan, 20 miles west of Ab-e-Garm on the Qazvin–Hamadan road, these hitherto unrecorded towers were discovered in the spring of 1965 by David Stronach, Director of the British Institute of Persian Studies, and T. Culyer Young, Jr, of the Royal Ontario Museum, while making a survey of Median and Achaemenian routes in western Persia. Both of these well-preserved, octagonal brick towers have rounded buttresses at each corner and resemble one another in plan, construction and decoration. Their exterior decorative brickwork is among the finest in Persia, including over a hundred separate patterns. The Kufic inscriptions are partly Koranic and partly historical, giving the date of the east tower (in the background) as 1067–68 and the other as 1093; they also indicate that both towers were the work of the same man. The east tower contains some internal frescoes, while both have double domes, the earliest known in Iran.

75 KANGAVAR, TEMPLE OF ANAHITA

A few fallen and broken Doric columns at Kangavar, half-way between Hamadan and Kermanshah, have long been identified with the once renowned temple of Anahita, probably built during the Seleucid period about 200 BC. Anahita, the Persian goddess of sacred waters, fertility and war, was worshipped by the Achaemenians in association with Mithras, the 'unconquerable Sun'. Her cult survived at least until Parthian times; under the Seleucids she was identified with the Aphrodite and Artemis of the Greeks.

In 1968 the Iranian Archaeological Service began to explore the western limits of the temple in preparation for more extensive campaigns in the years to come.

76 A WANDERING DERVISH

Two types of people are known as *'dervish'* in Persia. There are those who, as believers in religious mysticism, are members of one or other of the Sufi Orders which have long been a feature of Persian religious life and attract members from all classes of society. The other type is the wandering *dervish* – a 'seeker of truth' in the eyes of some, a 'religious tramp' and 'impostor' in the eyes of others. The wandering, mendicant *dervish*, now fast disappearing from the Persian scene, is almost invariably bearded and long-haired; he usually carries as a further mark of his calling a double-headed axe and a large begging bowl of metal or leather. This particular *dervish*, much less unkempt than most, was encountered in a Hamadan back street.

77 A KURDISH VILLAGER

This cheerful man is wearing the traditional Kurdish tassled turban. He comes from a village at the southern end of Lake Rezaiyeh.

The Kurdish tribal system is still strong, though not so much as it was. Many Kurds have long been permanently settled in villages, as is this man. But others still cling to their old nomadic ways and in the summer, with their flocks and household goods, move up from the plains to the mountain pastures, where they camp in black goat-hair tents.

78, 79 BAKHTIARIS

The Bakhtiaris are the largest and most purely Iranian of all the Persian tribes. They belong to the Lur race and their language is closely related to the oldest known forms of Persian. The annual Bakhtiari migration in April from their *garmsir*, or winter quarters in Khuzistan, to their *sardsir*, or summer pastures in the Chahar Mahal region of the plateau south-west of Isfahan, takes from four to six weeks. It is an epic of human courage and endurance in which men, women and children of all ages, with their animals and household goods, travel by five different migration routes across some of the wildest and most difficult mountain country in Persia in their search for grass.

The Bakhtiaris are divided into two major groups – the *Haft Lang* and the *Chahar Lang* – which in turn are divided into tribes, sub-tribes and clans. No one seems to know precisely how many Bakhtiaris there are in Persia; one estimate, which may be on the high side, is of 450,000, perhaps half being migratory and pastoral, the rest agricultural and settled.

The Bakhtiari man and girl shown here live permanently in the village of Karyak, about 120 miles south of Isfahan where the Kershan River, a tributary of the Karun, serves as the boundary between the Bakhtiari and Bor Ahmadi tribes.

Part Four THE CASPIAN AREA AND THE NORTH-EAST

81

82

84

85

88

89

94

95

97

98

103

104

106

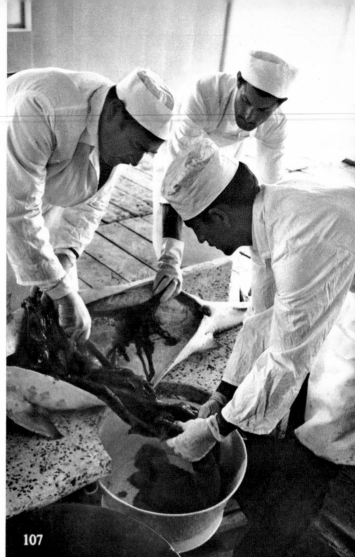

107

108

109

80 EASTERN ELBURZ MOUNTAINS

The transition from the bleak semi-desert of the central Persian plateau to the trees and lush green of the Caspian rain belt can be very abrupt, as those who have travelled from Tehran *via* Karaj and Chalus know. A more gradual approach is to motor north-east from Tehran to Shahrud, then, as illustrated here, through the cultivated and well-irrigated valleys of the eastern foothills of the Elburz Mountains to Shahpasand on the southern fringe of the Turkomen steppe.

81 TURKOMEN LADIES AT BANDAR SHAH

The Turkomens of the Gorgan steppe are one of the non-Persian peoples inhabiting Persia, first arriving there in the 11th century during the great Oghuz migration from central Asia. Their language is close to that of the Turks of Anatolia and similar to that spoken by the Uzbeks, Kazakhs and Turkomens of the USSR. They belong to two main tribes, the Yamut and Goklan, who live on the Turkomen or Gorgan steppe stretching north-eastwards from Bandar Shah, the port in the south-east corner of the Caspian Sea; the Atrek River separates them from their brother-Turkomens in the Soviet Republic of Turkmenistan. Until Reza Shah in the 1920s took steps to settle them, these Turkomens were nomads much feared for their plundering raids.

Note the Mongoloid slit eyes and high cheek-bones: also the bright headgear, consisting of red and dark green bands on a white ground; red is a favourite Turkomen colour, much used in their carpets.

82 TURKOMEN CHILDREN AND TENT AT PAHLEVI DEJ

Pahlevi Dej (formerly Ak Qaleh, or White Fort, in Turki) is a small market town in the heart of the Turkomen steppe, 12 miles north of Gorgan. Early each Thursday morning Yamut Turkomens from the surrounding countryside assemble there for the weekly market, a special feature being the horses and tribal rugs brought for sale.

83 TURKOMEN DWELLINGS AT PAHLEVI DEJ

As part of his policy of settling the unruly Turkomens, Reza Shah encouraged them to live in permanent houses such as the one illustrated. But old habits die slowly among tribal people, as can be seen here from the mud-made bread oven in the foreground and the tent next to the house. These circular tents with walls of matted reeds and roofs of felt and horse-hair, are similar to those of the Turki-speaking Shahsavan tribes of north-western Persia, but quite unlike the rectangular, black goat-hair tents of the Bakhtiari, Qashqai, and other nomadic or semi-nomadic tribes of the country.

84 KALAT-E-NADERI, THE DEFILE OF ARGHUN

Kalat-e-Naderi (Nadir's Fort) in north Khorassan, situated on the frontier with the USSR, is a remarkable natural fortress formed by a 50-mile circular wall of bare mountains, penetrable at only a few points. Curzon, who in 1889 failed to get past the Persian sentries guarding this Defile of Arghun, the principal entrance to the Kalat, described it as 'one of the most extraordinary natural phenomena in the world and famous even in this land of mountain fastnesses and impregnable defiles for its in-accessibility and amazing natural strength'. Although the Kalat is mentioned in Ferdowsi's 10th-century *Shah Nameh*, and withstood siege by Tamerlane, it was the 18th-century Persian conqueror of Delhi, Nadir Shah, who brought it fame when in 1741 he deposited there the spoils of his Indian campaign, including no doubt some of the crown jewels now on display in Tehran. They were probably stored in a curious octagonal pavilion, faced with richly decorated sandstone, which Nadir Shah built within the Kalat. He also built fortified watch-towers to cover all vulnerable points in the great rock wall and in places smoothed the rock so as to make it more difficult to scale. *From a colour photograph by Denis Wright.*

85 VILLAGE OF NAU DEH NEAR BUJNURD

In order to protect his country from Turkomen raiders, Shah Abbas I, in the early 17th century, moved a number of Kurdish tribes, notably the Shadlu, Zafaranlu and Keyvanlu from Ardalan in western Persia to north Khorassan, to settle and serve as wardens of his north-eastern marches. Bujnurd is still the headquarters of the Shadlu, and is surrounded by Kurdish villages such as Nau Deh (New Village), whose compact, flat-roofed mud houses, ranged in terraces, resemble the mountain villages of Kurdistan proper.

The Kurds of Khorassan have, however, lost virtually all contact with their cousins in the west of Persia: they no longer wear the Kurdish national dress, nor do they speak true Kurdish. They have mostly abandoned the Sunni for the Shi'a faith.

86 YAMUT TURKOMEN

This old man of the steppes wears the traditional black sheepskin Turkomen hat. His wispy fringe of beard is typical of the facial style of the older generation of Turkomen, whose sons, however, prefer to be clean-shaven and to dress in western habit. The *tesbih*, or string of beads, in his hand serves as a rosary, being carried by Sunnis and Shi'ites alike.

87–92 MESHED, SHRINE OF THE IMAM REZA AND THE MOSQUE OF GAWHAR SHAD

The vast majority of Persia's 27 million people are Shi'a Moslems of the Jafari code. The basic difference between them and Sunni Moslems, the other great division of Islam, concerns the true succession to the Prophet Mohammed. The Sunnis recognize the authority of the first three elected Caliphs, the Shi'as only that of the direct descendants of the Prophet and his son-in-law, Ali (Mohammed had no son), known as the Twelve Imams, of whom the last mysteriously disappeared in AD 873 and will, according to Shi'ite legend, reappear on the Day of Judgment in the Gawhar Shad Mosque at Meshed.

Reza, the Eighth Imam, is the only one of the Twelve to be buried in Persia. Hence the fact that Meshed, where he is buried, is the holiest city in Persia and ranks next to the Iraqi towns of Nejef and Kerbala, where the first and third Imams are buried, as a Shi'ite pilgrim centre. It is very rare for infidels to be allowed into the shrine.

The story is that the Imam Reza, while travelling in Khorassan with his father-in-law, the Caliph Mamun, suddenly died in 817 at Sanabad, where they were spending the night. Mamun's father, Harun-al-Rashid, the most famous of the Abbasid Caliphs, had himself died and been buried at Sanabad in 809. The Imam Reza was buried next to him and the place renamed Meshed-ar-Rizawi, *i.e.* the place of the martyrdom of Reza, since it was suspected that he had been poisoned. The Imam's reputed piety and miraculous powers, together with a Shi'ite belief that the Prophet himself had declared that a part of his body would be buried in Khorassan, soon attracted pilgrims to his grave, though it was not until the Safavids in the 16th century adopted Shi'ism as the national religion, that Meshed came into its own as a great pilgrim centre.

Much of the original 9th-century shrine over the Imam's grave was destroyed in the following century; it was rebuilt by Sultan Mahmud of Gazni in 1009, but severely damaged by the Mongols in the 12th century and bombarded by the Russians in 1912. Sultan Oljeitu of Sultaniyeh fame (Plate VIII) embellished the shrine in the early 14th century, as did Shah Rukh, the son of Timur (Tamerlane), a century later, and Shahs Abbas I, Nadir, Fath Ali and Nasr-ud-din in succeeding centuries. The result of so much royal and private benefaction is, to quote Pope, that 'perhaps there is no other group of buildings in the world which give such an effect of opulence. A gold dome, two gold minarets, two huge gold *ivans*, massive silver and gilt doors. . . .' But the desire to embellish and modernize has not always been for the best; in particular much beautiful tilework has been sacrificed in favour of gaudy mirror-work.

Gawhar Shad, the wife of the Mongol ruler Shah Rukh, built this beautiful mosque between 1405 and 1418 immediately to the south of the shrine: though within the shrine's precincts it is technically and legally separate. Sir Percy Sykes, soldier, diplomat and historian, describes it as 'the noblest mosque in Central Asia', and Pope as 'the first and the greatest surviving Persian monument of the 15th century'. The façade of its four-*ivan* court (314 by 277 ft.) is decorated with brilliant mosaic tiling of the highest quality; the two storeys of arcaded rooms round the court are used for religious teaching and gatherings. Behind the *ivan* can be seen the shrine's golden dome and minaret.

89 The Old Court (Sahn-e-Kohneh)

Pilgrims are assembling for evening prayer and are turning to face the dazzling 15th-century golden *ivan*.

Of the shrine's two main courtyards, the 480-ft.-long Old Court dates from Safavid times and the New Court, to the south-east, from early Qajar times. Both courts have the usual four *ivans* and a two-storeyed arcaded façade decorated with polychrome tiles; the upper storey rooms in this court are allocated to distinguished Persian scholars for life and those on the ground floor are used as private chapels where verses from the Koran are daily recited in memory of the dead.

90 Shrine doorkeeper

A doorkeeper in modern uniform stands guardian at each entrance to the shrine. He holds, as a symbol of office, a silver mace, or *chomaq*, which a pilgrim reverently touches: his job is to maintain law and order.

91 Entrance to the Chamber of Felicity (Dar-ol-Sa'adeh)

The *Haram*, or tomb chamber of the Imam, is reached through a complex of rooms and passages, of which this is one. Dazzling 19th-century mirror-work is the main feature of the ante-chamber to the Dar-ol-Sa'adeh. On the left is a great door of finely chased silver which wailing pilgrims, often worked into a state of near-hysteria by their religious fervour as they approach the *Haram*, fondle and kiss.

92 Evening in the New Court (Sahn-e-Nau)

Night and day the shrine is never empty of pilgrims; it is reliably estimated that well over a million of them visit the shrine annually, drawn mainly from Iran, Iraq, Afghanistan and Pakistan.

Here, beyond Fath Ali Shah's sumptuous gold *ivan*, can be seen the tomb chamber's golden dome and minaret. The dome, probably built in the early 14th century, was redecorated by command of Shah Abbas I at the beginning of the 17th century, when its tiles of gilded copper plate were renovated by the court goldsmith in Isfahan.

The tall building to the right is the entrance portal to the Old Court and dates from the reign of Shah Abbas I; the small pavilion on top is known as a *Nakkara Khaneh* (Drum Tower), the last of its kind in Persia, where each morning and evening a drum and trumpet tattoo is played. The gold minaret to its left was originally built by Shah Tahmasp, but reconstructed in the 18th century.

93 BASTAM, SHRINE OF BAYAZID AL-BASTAMI

Bayazid al-Bastami, also known as Sheikh Abu Yazid, was a famous Sufi saint who died in 874 and was buried at Bastam, 8 miles from Shahrud. In the course of time a jumble of religious buildings, most of them dating from 1299–1313, grew up round this sacred spot, which became and has remained a popular place of pilgrimage.

The Seljuk minaret seen here is dated 1120 and the two tiled *ivans* 1313. Bayazid's tomb is in the right-hand corner: behind it is a tomb chamber decorated with good 14th-century stucco work.

There is a further group of religious buildings, including the Friday Mosque and an early 14th-century fluted tomb tower, a few hundred yards to the south.

94 QABUS'S TOMB TOWER (GONBAD-E-QABUS)

It is difficult in a single photograph to do justice to what is undoubtedly the most beautiful as well as the earliest and simplest tomb tower in Persia. Robert Byron, who decided to visit Persia after seeing Diez's picture of it, ranked Gonbad-e-Qabus with the great buildings of the world; Pope describes it as 'a supreme architectural masterpiece'.

The tower stands on an artificial mound at the northern end of the bustling Turkomen market town named after it, about 70 miles north-east of Gorgan. It is visible from miles away across the flat steppe and is all that remains of Jurgan, the old provincial capital of the Ziyarid princes, one of whom was the gifted Shams al Ma'ali Qabus. He ruled there between 976 and 1012 and caused his tomb to be built during his own lifetime, as the two Kufic inscriptions around it record. It was completed in 1006. Built entirely of fired brick, it consists of a cylindrical tower 167 ft. high, supported and decorated by ten buttresses and crowned with a conical roof for which bricks were specially made. A single opening on the east side gives access to the interior, which is empty and devoid of decoration, thus lending support to the tradition that Qabus's body was suspended in a glass coffin from the roof.

95 DAMAGHAN, TOMB TOWER OF PIR-E-ALAMDAR
(GONBAD-E-PIR-E-ALAMDAR). DETAIL

While Gonbad-e-Qabus (Plate 94) is the earliest of some fifty tomb towers still extant in Persia, that of Pir-e-Alamdar, dated 1027, at Damghan is the oldest south of the Elburz Mountains. Like most such towers it is round and built entirely of brick, which has been used with excellent effect in the outset decorative bands, including one of Kufic script below the squat dome, producing, in Pope's words, 'a variety of surface which the Seljuks subtleized but never surpassed'.

Pir-e-Alamdar is said to have been the father of a local Governor of Damghan.

96 DAMGHAN, TARI KHANEH. QIBLA WALL ARCADE

This ruined mosque at Damghan, probably built in the third quarter of the 8th century, is the oldest Islamic building in Persia and marks an important transition from Sassanian to Islamic architecture. Many writers name it the *Tarik Khaneh,* or Dark House, others prefer *Tari Khaneh* (God's House), *tari* being an old Turkish word for God. It is also known as the Mosque of the Forty Columns and is designed according to the simple Arabian plan, *i.e.* an almost square open court surrounded by tunnel-vaulted arcades. The deepest arcade, on the *qibla* wall side, is supported by three rows of massive round piers over 5 ft. in diameter. The use of brick in the construction of the piers was one of the Sassanian techniques employed in this building.

97 MAZANDERAN PROVINCE, VILLAGE HOUSE NEAR BABOLSAR

The domestic architecture of the Caspian provinces of Gilan and Mazanderan is quite different from that found elsewhere in Persia, where most houses have flat roofs and are built of brick, very often unfired, covered with plaster. Because of the heavy rainfall, houses on the northern side of the Elburz Mountains in the Caspian rainbelt have sloping roofs made of thatch, wooden shingles or burnt tiles, and are built of wood or fired brick. However, as can be seen in this illustration, the traditional *talar*, or columned porch, is maintained. Water is no problem and most houses have their own wells.

98 MAZANDERAN PROVINCE, BANDAR SHAH. TURKOMEN WOMEN ROLLING FELT

The Turkomens make much use of felt, particularly as roofing and floor covering for their tents, and as saddle cloths for their horses. Elsewhere in Persia, specially shaped hats such as those worn by the Bakhtiari and Qashqai tribesmen, as well as shepherds' cloaks, are made of felt.

The art of making felt, a woven or matted textile usually of wool, is older than that of weaving and still flourishes in many parts of Persia, particularly in tribal areas. It is a fascinating sight to watch felt-makers at work in the bazaars. Their skill is such that they can, without benefit of mechanical equipment, produce complete cloaks with sleeves and hood in one piece, as well as decorate rugs with fulled-in patterns of dyed wool. The rolling process illustrated here lasts several hours and is designed to compact and straighten out the newly-made felt so that it will lie flat.

99 MARKET DAY IN A CASPIAN TOWN

In the smaller Persian towns, especially on market days, pavements are much used by itinerant vendors to show off their wares. The little bags on display here contain a variety of nuts, seeds and dried fruits, known collectively as *ajil*, which are eaten before and after meals in most Persian homes.

The pistachio, grown principally in the Rafsinjan–Kerman area of south-east Persia, is the most popular nut, though walnuts, almonds and hazel nuts are also eaten: so too is melon seed, which has first to be adroitly split with the teeth to extract the edible kernel. The main dried fruits composing *ajil* are raisins, mulberries, apricots and figs.

100 NORTH-WEST KHORASSAN, COTTON PICKING AT ASH KHANEH

Cotton is Persia's major industrial crop and is grown in various parts of the country. The best cotton, some being of the long-staple upland American variety, is produced in the Gorgan and north-west Khorassan regions, where it is grown on a large scale. Production of unginned cotton during recent years has been between 300,000 and 400,000 tons anually.

Persian cotton first appeared in foreign markets at the time of the American Civil War. Today, as a result of the introduction of better varieties and marketing techniques, a considerable export trade has developed, nearly a third of the annual crop being exported – mainly to the USSR and Eastern Europe, but also to Western Europe where the UK has been the largest importer in recent years: the balance is absorbed by domestic cotton mills at Isfahan, Tehran, Yazd, Shahi and Kashan.

101 PREPARING STRAW FOR THATCHING NEAR SHAHSAVAR (MAZANDERAN)

The circulating horses are straightening and flattening out the rice straw, which is then sold to thatchers who are much in demand in the Caspian area to provide roofing for houses and barns.

Similarly, where modern threshing techniques have not yet been introduced, threshing of rice, wheat and other grains is done by the antique method of a pair of draft animals being driven round and round a hardened earthen threshing floor, usually drawing behind them a flint-studded threshing board or a wain armed with rotating wooden or iron beaters.

102 WINNOWING RICE NEAR BANDAR GAZ

Rice of excellent quality is the principal crop of the Caspian provinces. It is also grown on a smaller scale in various other parts of Persia and is the staple of most meals: it is the basis of the national dish, *chelau kebab*, and of all *pilaus*. Despite the rapid mechanization of agriculture in recent years, hand winnowing is still practised in many parts as it has been for generations. The threshed grain is thrown into the air on wooden shovels or pronged forks so that the wind may carry the chaff and husks away while the grain, being heavier, falls to the ground.

103 FISHING ON THE MORDAB NEAR BANDAR PAHLEVI

Mordab (Dead Water) is the name given to the various shallow lagoons on the Persian shores of the Caspian Sea. The largest of these, part river, part swamp, lies between Bandar Pahlevi (formerly Enzeli) and Rasht, 25 miles inland. In places where the reeds are thick, channels are kept clear through which boats can be rowed or punted.

Wild fowl and fish abound in the *Mordab*, both being caught in nets by experienced local hunters working from boats – the fish, as shown here, by a weighted net which is flung out into the water and then, as it sinks, closes on the fish; duck by a combination of drum, light and net, used from a boat moving across the waters at night. A monotonous drum-beat serves to blanket out other sounds that might alarm the duck. A dim light helps the hunter spot the duck which he catches with a net at the end of a long pole.

104 GILAN PROVINCE, CORMORANTS ON THE BANKS OF THE SEFID RUD

Cormorants as well as an enormous variety of wild fowl and waders – swans, geese, ducks, herons, curlews, shanks, sandpipers, etc. – frequent the Caspian provinces of Gilan and Mazanderan, especially the vast *Mordab* swamp between Bandar Pahlevi and Rasht. Some are permanent, others winter residents only, most being migrants from the north flying south in their tens of thousands to Arabia and Africa in the autumn and returning in the spring.

105 SEFID RUD VALLEY, PADDY FIELDS

The Sefid Rud (White River) is one of the three main rivers draining large areas of Persia into the Caspian Sea; it breaks through the Elburz Mountains south of Rasht, then divides into numerous channels which find their way across the coastal plain to the sea east of Bandar Pahlevi. Rice is the main crop grown in the river's wide valley.

This photograph was taken in the autumn. The rice has been harvested and, with only the stubble remaining, it is easier to notice the elaborate system of irrigation channels whereby water from the river is distributed by force of gravity to flood the small paddy fields. Successful rice cultivation demands abundant water and a hot climate, both of which exist north of the Elburz Mountains in the Caspian provinces. Tea is another important crop in certain parts of the region. In 1967–68 about 912,000 tons of rice and 63,000 tons of tea were harvested in Persia.

172

106–109 CAVIAR

The finest caviar in the world comes from Persia thanks to the quality of the sturgeon (whose roe it is) which frequent the Persian or southern shores of the Caspian Sea.

For years – between 1893 and 1928 – the Russians held a concession, granted by the Persian government originally to a Russian subject named Lianasoff, to exploit these valuable fisheries. Fishing stations, refrigerating and processing plant were set up on the Caspian shore to prepare the caviar and other fish products for export to Russia. In 1928 the Russian monopoly was broken with the granting of a 25-year concession to a joint Irano-Soviet fishing company; and in 1953, when that concession ended, a 100 per cent Persian Government-owned company took over, with headquarters in the old Russian buildings at Bandar Pahlevi. Even today, however, the USSR buys about a third of Persia's annual caviar production.

106 BELUGA STURGEON

Of the five varieties of sturgeon found in the Caspian the three most valuable commercially are known as the Great Sturgeon (or Beluga), the plain Sturgeon (Oscietre) and the Starry Sturgeon (Sevruga). The largest is the Beluga which averages between 165 and 220 lbs. in weight, 6½ and 8 ft. in length, and yields between 37 and 44 lbs. of caviar. The smaller Oscietre and Sevruga yield between 9 and 15 lbs. and 3 and 4½ lbs. respectively of caviar. It is said that the really big Beluga sometimes caught may be as much as 100 years old and that the average age of those caught is about 40.

As a rule the bigger sturgeon are fished all the year round, the best months being March/April and September/October. They are caught either on long lines armed with an array of hooks or in nets, both lines and nets being fixed fairly close in-shore and then dragged in. The fish are taken to the nearest processing station along the shore as soon as possible after being caught since it is important to extract the caviar without delay.

107 EXTRACTING THE CAVIAR

The sturgeon has been split open with a large knife within minutes of arriving at the processing station, and its roe quickly removed.

108 PROCESSING CAVIAR

Caviar is sold and eaten raw; before being put into tins it is cleansed and a preservative added – for the American market this consists of salt while for the European and Persian market boric acid and borax is mixed with the salt.

109 BELUGA CAVIAR

There are various qualities of caviar. The connoisseur will immediately recognize this as being Beluga caviar of the highest quality. The bigger the grain and the lighter the colour, the better. Small-grain caviar is black; the larger grains are either grey or yellowish in colour; the latter, known as 'golden caviar', is rare and is reserved for the use of the royal family and their guests.

The best caviar is packed and sold in round tins such as this, in various sizes; lower-quality 'pressed' caviar is exported in barrels. Apart from 40 tons consumed locally the entire 220 tons of caviar produced in the Persian year 1967–68 was exported – 70 tons to the USSR, 60 tons to the USA and 50 tons to Europe.

Part Five   TEHRAN AND MODERN PERSIA

112

113

117

118

119

121

120

122

123

124

126

127

128

131

132

133

135

138

110 TEHRAN, GULESTAN PALACE. CORONATION HALL AND FORMER MUSEUM

Agha Mohammed Khan, the first of the Qajars, made Tehran his capital in 1788. His successor, Fath Ali Shah, completed the Gulestan Palace, which was one of a group of royal buildings then enclosed within mud walls known as the *Arg*. Nasr-ud-din Shah, influenced by what he had seen during his first European tour in 1873, added a Museum in the form of a large, first-floor hall decorated with mirror work, where some of the priceless Crown Jewels (now beautifully displayed in the vaults of the National Bank) were put on show side by side with what Curzon described as 'unutterable rubbish', much of it acquired by Nasr-ud-din Shah on his European tours.

The Coronation of Reza Khan and his son, Mohammed Reza Pahlevi, both took place in this fine hall. Before Reza Khan's Coronation on 25 April 1926, Mrs Harold Nicolson (Miss Vita Sackville-West, the writer), wife of the then Counsellor at the British Legation in Tehran, undertook the re-arrangement of the Museum. Before the present Shah's Coronation on 26 October 1967, the hall was completely renovated and redecorated under the direction of the well-known Persian architect, Senator Mohsen Foroughi.

The Shah holds New Year and Birthday Salaams in the Coronation Hall, where Ministers, foreign Ambassadors and other dignitaries in full dress offer their congratulations to the *Shahanshah*, the King of Kings.

Queen Elizabeth II and Prince Philip stayed in a specially built modern wing of the Gulestan Palace during their State Visit to Persia in 1961, as various other State visitors have done since.

111–113 MODERN PERSIAN ARCHITECTURE

The westernization of Persia was begun by Reza Shah, and reflected itself to some extent in the rather ponderous public buildings erected in Tehran during his reign. It was not until after the economic and political disruptions caused by World War II and the Anglo-Iranian oil dispute that a building boom, coupled with a rapid expansion in the population of Tehran, provided an opportunity for young Iranian architects, trained in London and Paris as well as in Tehran, to apply their knowledge of western architectural styles and building techniques to the Persian scene. The result has been astounding and has all but transformed Tehran within a decade from a city of essentially oriental aspect into one whose buildings might be those of a modern European or South American city.

111 HEADQUARTERS OF THE NATIONAL IRANIAN OIL COMPANY

The National Iranian Oil Company was established immediately after the nationalization of the oil industry in March 1951 as an autonomous State body with responsibility for the development of Persia's enormous oil resources. It is fitting that the headquarters of Persia's major industry should be Tehran's most impressive office block which, when completed in 1961, was the tallest building in the capital. It was also the first large building to be constructed of reinforced concrete and shows the characteristics of this type of structure, duly modified to suit local requirements, *e.g.*, since Persia suffers from extremely high temperatures during the summer months, the architect, Paris-trained Mr Aziz Farman Farmaian, has cantilevered the floors to provide protection by shading.

Red double-decker Leyland buses, such as the one shown here, are a common sight in Tehran: some 250 of them were imported from Britain between 1958 and 1960. Now they are assembled and part-manufactured in Tehran.

112 THE SENATE

The Iranian Parliament consists of an Upper and Lower House, the Senate and the Majlis, who until the completion of this building in 1960 shared accommodation in an old Qajar building next to the Sepah Salar mosque (Plate 121).

The architect, Mr Mohsen Foroughi, son of a famous Prime Minister and himself now a Senator, was the first Persian to study architecture in Europe. Both he and his collaborator on this building, Mr Ghiai, were trained in Paris. Their symmetrical Senate is highly original and modern in style, though the traditional *talar* portico is retained in the tall columns of white Italian marble in the recessed wings. The rectilinear central façade protects the main building from the fierce midday sun, towards which it is orientated, while the broad steps below provide a worthy approach to this important building which offers ample space, as well as much comfort, to Persia's sixty Senators.

Each autumn the Shah, accompanied by the Empress and members of the Royal Family, drives in state to the Senate to open the new parliamentary session.

113 TABRIZ, 25TH OF SHAHRIVAR RAILWAY STATION. ENTRANCE

A solid reinforced concrete structure best describes this big railway station at Tabriz. It was designed by a French architect, M. F. Pouillon, built by Cementation Ltd, a British firm, and opened in 1958. There is an identical station at Meshed. Neither

198

of the stations yet have the volume of railway traffic that their size would seem to merit. The 25th of Shahrivar (16th of September) is the anniversary of the Shah's accession to the throne in 1941.

Until Reza Shah's reign there were no long-distance railway lines in Persia. Thanks largely to his personal initiative the 860-mile-long Trans-Iranian line from Bandar Shapur, at the head of the Persian Gulf, via Tehran to Bandar Shah on the south-east shore of the Caspian, was begun in 1927 and completed in 1938. His next project, a north-west line from Tehran to Tabriz, was interrupted by World War II and not finished until 1958. From Tabriz a line links up with the Soviet railway system at Julfa. Soon there will also be a direct link between Tabriz and the Turkish railway system.

114 SKI SLOPES AT AB-ALI

Skiing has become immensely popular in Persia, encouraged by the fact that both the Shah and Empress are first-class skiers often to be seen on the slopes near Tehran.

The first ski-lifts seen in Persia were installed after World War II at Ab-Ali, about 40 miles by road east of Tehran, which is still a popular ski resort despite the counter-attractions of the longer and steeper slopes at Shemshak, about 35 miles north of the capital. A big new ski resort is in process of being built in the Elburz Mountains.

The skiing season usually lasts from late December until March or April.

115 MOUNT DEMAVAND

Demavand, 45 miles north-east of Tehran, is the highest mountain in Persia, its 18,550-ft. snow-capped volcanic cone being a landmark for miles around, often visible from Tehran.

A young Englishman, W. T. Thomson, who as Sir William Thomson was H.M. Minister in Tehran from 1872 to 1879, was the first European to climb the mountain in 1836 – a long steady grind rather than a mountaineering feat.

The river in the foreground is a tributary of the River Lar, which curls round Demavand before cutting its way through a deep gorge below Pulur to the Caspian. In the summer the upper Lar Valley is dotted with the black tents of nomads who remain there with their sheep and goats until early September. The river, soon to be dammed to provide more water for Tehran's expanding population, is a trout fisherman's paradise much favoured by generations of British diplomats who annually each summer have set up camp there on the same site where Miss Gertrude Bell records having camped with members of the British Legation in 1892.

116 PULUR VILLAGE, WINTER LANDSCAPE

Pulur lies under the shadow of Mount Demavand, about 55 miles by road north-east of Tehran on the old caravan track to Amol and the Caspian Sea. Reza Shah planned to build a motor road along this route but it got no further than Pulur before the outbreak of World War II. It was not until July 1963 that this important road, the shortest between Tehran and the Caspian, was opened by the present Shah.

A succession of fifteen rock-cut tunnels enables the road to follow the Haraz River, as the Lar is called in its lower reaches, down its steep gorge from Pulur through the Elburz. The mountain scenery on the road is magnificent.

117 TEHRAN, GATEWAY OF THE NATIONAL GARDENS (DARVAZEH-YE-BAGH-E-MELLI), FROM THE SOUTH

This imposing brick gateway, decorated with *haft rangi* tiles, was built in 1922 by command of Reza Khan when he was Minister of War. It faces what is still the Ministry of War, an old Qajar building a few hundred yards to the north; the space between was for many years a big military parade ground, the Maidan-e-Mashq, but has now been built over. On the right through the gateway are the large police headquarters, built in neo-Achaemenian style during Reza Shah's reign; on the left a new museum completed in 1967, and the Ministry for Foreign Affairs.

Apart from numerous faience inscriptions, the tiling on both sides of the gateway illustrates military subjects such as machine guns and soldiers. The main faience inscription over the central arch, which is crowned by a chamber where military music was played, is in Arabic and records well-known words of the Prophet Mohammed as quoted by the Imam Reza. Another inscription states that the gateway's wrought-iron work was made in the Tehran arsenal.

118 SHAHR-E-REY, SHRINE OF SHAH ABDUL AZIM. NORTH-EAST FAÇADE

The shrine of Shah Abdul Azim (Shah being a religious title) at Rey, 7 miles south-east of Tehran, ranks after those at Meshed and Qum as a Persian pilgrim centre. Three important religious figures of the Shi'ite world are buried, each under his own domed chamber, within this complex of buildings – Abdul Azim, a martyred great-grandson of the Second Imam Hassan; Hamzeh, brother of the Eighth Imam; and Taher, descendant of the Fourth Imam.

Abdul Azim's body lies buried beneath the golden dome illustrated here. Although this, as well as the tiled minarets and mirror-work within the *ivan*, dates from the 19th century, the columned façade belongs to the Safavid period.

Persia's first railway line was built by a Belgian syndicate to carry pilgrims from Tehran to the shrine. Nasr-ud-din Shah, who inaugurated the railway in 1888, was himself assassinated when leaving the shrine eight years later and lies buried with others of his line within its precincts.

In 1905–06, during the great constitutional struggle, hundreds of political refugees sought *bast* or sanctuary within these grounds.

The sanctity conferred on Rey by the shrine is responsible for its popularity as a burial place; many Tehranis maintain family mausoleums there, and Reza Shah, who died in exile in South Africa in 1944, is buried close to the shrine within a massive tomb where it is customary for newly-accredited ambassadors as well as distinguished visitors to lay a wreath.

Rey, the ancient Rhages, was devastated by the Mongols in 1220 and has never regained its former importance. Today it is virtually a suburb of Tehran.

119 TEHRAN, ROYAL HUNTING LODGE AT FARAHABAD

The eastern suburbs of Tehran now stretch as far as Doshan Tepeh (Hare's Hill) and Farahabad (Abode of Joy), a royal hunting ground of both the Qajars and the Pahlevis on the edge of the desert. Little trace remains today of the palace and zoological gardens Nasr-ud-din Shah built there, but Muzaffar-ud-din Shah's (1896–1907) curious three-storeyed, circular hunting lodge, illustrated here, is still occasionally used by members of the Royal Family and their guests. It was completed in 1904 and is said to have been modelled after the Trocadero Palace in Paris. The circular and lofty entrance hall sparkles with mirror-work. The lodge contains some fine Persian carpets, and European paintings and ornaments of an earlier age, as well as two stuffed tigers shot by the present Shah in India.

The royal stables are also housed at Farahabad. The wide expanse of desert and mountain between Farahabad and the Jaje River a few miles to the north-east, these days more a royal game reserve than a hunting ground, is marvellously unspoiled, despite its proximity to Tehran; wild mountain sheep and goats, as well as leopard, wander here at will.

120 TEHRAN, RESIDENCE OF THE BRITISH AMBASSADOR

Built in 1869–70 to the design of Mr J. W. Wild of the South Kensington Museum, London, and under the supervision of a Captain Pierson and one NCO on the staff of the Indian Telegraph Company, the British Ambassador's Residence, together with offices and staff houses, is situated within a 15-acre compound in the heart of Tehran. When built, however, it was in the desert outside the city walls. With its lawns, gardens and huge plane trees it is one of the most impressive as well as one of the more individualis-tic Embassies in the Middle East, and it has been the scene of historic occasions. In the summer of 1906 some 12,000 Tehranis took *bast*, or sanctuary, for nearly three weeks within the Embassy compound and by thus disrupting the life of the city were able to force Muzaffar-ud-din Shah to meet their demands for constitutional reform. On 30 November 1943, during the Tehran Conference, Winston Churchill, with President Roosevelt and Marshal Stalin as his principal guests, celebrated his 69th birthday in the Residence at a dinner party which he described in his War Memoirs as 'a memorable occasion in my life'. Two silver plaques in the magnificent State dining room record the occasion.

The 'pagoda' on top is purely ornamental in intent. It can be reached only by climbing over the roof. The three-arched entrance to the Residence was added in 1964 when the private wing (not visible) was rebuilt.

121 TEHRAN, SOUTH-WEST IVAN OF THE MOSQUE OF THE COMMANDER-IN-CHIEF (MASJID-E-SEPAH SALAR)

Serving both as a mosque and a theological college, the Sepah Salar with its eight minarets is the largest and most important mosque in Tehran, where State funerals are held. It is situated in the centre of the town immediately south of the old Majlis building and is a haven of tranquillity from the noisy traffic outside.

Built on the traditional four-*ivan* plan round a large, arcaded, two-storey court, the mosque was not completed until 1890. Funds for its construction were provided by the enormously rich Mirza Hussein Khan, who had been in turn Nasr-ud-din Shah's Grand Vizier, Minister for Foreign Affairs and Commander-in-Chief.

The south-west *ivan* shown here leads into the spacious domed sanctuary chamber which has been retiled, in and outside, during recent years and now provides an excellent example of contemporary Persian tilework, both *haft rangi* and mosaic. The north-east *ivan* opposite is surmounted by a tiled clock-tower and flanked by a pair of small minarets.

122 TEHRAN, SOUTH IVAN OF THE ROYAL MOSQUE (MASJID-E-SHAH)

Fath Ali Shah, who did much to embellish his newly founded capital, began building this mosque about 1809; it was not finished until 1840 and stands at the northern entrance to the bazaar not far from the Gulestan Palace; two side entrances lead directly into the bazaar.

The mosque has the usual four *ivans*, on each of the four sides of a single-storey arcaded court, decorated with early 19th-century *haft rangi* tiles. The turquoise and white dome of the sanctuary chamber beyond the south *ivan* is crowned by a small gilded cupola seen here peeping over the *ivan*.

At the pool in the centre of the court – a feature of nearly all mosques – the faithful are performing their ritual ablutions before midday prayer.

123 TEHRAN BAZAAR, CARPET REPAIRER

Every Persian town of any size has a carpet section in its bazaar. The carpet bazaar in Tehran is perhaps the biggest of its kind in the world. Carpets and rugs from all over Persia, of every sort, size and quality, are assembled there, many for export and others for sale locally.

There are hundreds of Tehran *bazaaris* – many of them originally from Tabriz – dealing in carpets in one way or another. Many others, following the present drift away from the bazaars, have opened carpet shops in various parts of Tehran, the biggest concentration being in Ferdowsi Avenue opposite the British Embassy, where most of the dealers in carpets and antiques are members of Persia's ancient Jewish community.

Here the finishing touches are being given to a repair job done in the bazaar.

124 TEHRAN BAZAAR, GREENGROCER'S STALL

A great variety of fruits and vegetables of excellent quality are grown in Persia – cherries, apricots, peaches, strawberries, melons, grapes, figs, apples, oranges, grapefruit, pome-granates, etc., as well as all the familiar European vegetables. The courgettes and small cucumbers shown in the foreground are particularly popular and, to the surprise of newly-arrived Europeans, the latter are usually served with and eaten raw as fruit at the end of a meal.

125 TEHRAN, SAMOVARS FOR SALE

The habit of drinking tea, the national beverage of Persia, is relatively new, having been introduced – in company with the samovar – from Russia in the 19th century during the reign of Nasr-ud-din Shah. Previously coffee, brought to Persia by the Arabs, had been the popular drink in a land where religion forbade the drinking of wine and spirits.

Few Persian families are without their samovar, in which water is kept on the boil ready to replenish the teapot placed on top when not in use. About half a million samovars are manufactured annually in Persia these days, mostly in small factories but some still by hand in the bazaars. The samovar-makers of Borujerd in Luristan are particularly renowned.

126 TEHRAN, RUDAKI HALL

The completion of the Rudaki Hall in 1967, nearly ten years in the building, filled a major gap in Tehran's cultural life by providing a modern opera house and concert hall equipped with the very latest theatrical and electrical devices. The hall – built under the auspices of the Ministry of Fine Arts and Culture – is named after the blind

10th-century poet, Rudaki, 'the first great classical poet of Persia', and provides accommodation for audiences of up to 1,350 as well as permanent quarters for the National School of Ballet. The architect was a Persian Armenian, Dr Eugene Aftandilian, who studied in Paris.

The floodlit marble entrance foyer seen here incorporates the traditional *talar* motif. Behind, towers the mass of the main building. By contrast to the Hall's overpowering vertical exterior, its horseshoe theatre within has the cosy, white-and-gold, red-plush air of a 19th-century European opera house, complete with two tiers of boxes and gallery above.

The Shah and Empress, together with members of the Royal Family, Cabinet Ministers and Ambassadors attended a gala opening of the Hall on the evening of the Shah's Coronation on 26 October 1967, when two short Persian operas and national folk-dances were performed. Since then a succession of world-famous international artistes have appeared in the Rudaki Hall before packed houses. On one memorable evening, in October 1968, Margot Fonteyn and Nureyev danced there to the violin of Yehudi Menuhin.

127 TEHRAN, BELLY DANCER

Tehran has a lively night life, ranging from sophisticated cabarets, where top European artistes perform, and densely packed discothèques which would not be out of place in London or Paris, to truly Persian shows performed by Persian dancers, singers and acrobats. Despite its name, the *Moulin Rouge*, where this photograph was taken, is essentially Persian in character and caters for a Persian clientèle which never tires of a good belly dancer.

128 TEHRAN, JAFFARY'S ZURKHANEH

Zurkhanehs (Houses of Strength), or gymnastic clubs, are a peculiarly Persian institution found nowhere else in the Middle East. Their history is lost in the past; they may have come into being at the time of the Arab invasions when they served both as gymnasiums and as secret meeting-places where the national spirit was kept alive.

A *Zurkhaneh*, with its disciplines and grades, has been compared to a Masonic Lodge. A youth joins as a *Nowcheh* (Novice) and, as he masters the traditional exercises, graduates to the rank of *Pish Kesvat* (Trained Athlete), ultimately aspiring to become a *Pahlavan Akbar* (First Champion) who leads the exercises. These follow a ritual in all *Zurkhanehs* and are accompanied by a *Morshed* (Director), using drum and bell, who chants verses from Ferdowsi's *Shah Nameh*, the 10th-century Persian epic. Heavy Indian clubs, wooden shields, steel bows and chains – refinements of ancient weapons – are used in some of the exercises, which are performed in a pit, square or hexagonal, known as the *Gowd*, over which hangs a picture of the Imam Ali, the patron saint of *Zurkhanehs*.

In Tehran the two best known *Zurkhanehs* are those of the Bank Melli and of a private owner, Sha'ban Jaffary, both of which have become tourist attractions.

129 AMIR KABIR (KARAJ) DAM, HIGH TENSION WIRES AND DAM FACE

The settlement in 1954 of the costly Anglo-Iranian oil dispute resulted in a steady and spectacular increase in Persia's oil revenues which, from the Oil Consortium alone, rose from £35.5 million in 1955 to £336.3 million in 1968. Most of this revenue – 80 per cent in 1968 – has been allocated to the financing of successive and ambitious Seven Year Plans for economic and social development which are rapidly transforming the face of Persia. Under the second Seven Year Plan, launched in 1955, work was begun on three large dams at Dez, Karaj and Manjil, designed to provide water and electric power over wide areas.

The 590 ft. high, double-curvature arch dam near Karaj is about 40 miles north-west of Tehran on the road to Chalus. Built by American consultants and contractors, it was opened by the Shah in October 1961, and supplies electric power (85,000 kw. capacity) and industrial and drinking water for Tehran, previously dependent on *qanats* (Plate 52) and the water cart for this vital necessity.

Amir Kabir, after whom the dam is named, was Nasr-ud-din Shah's reformist Grand Vizier, murdered in the royal gardens at Fin (Plate 58) in 1852.

130 EMPRESS FARAH (MANJIL) DAM

Situated in Gilan province at Manjil on the Qazvin-Rasht road, where the Shah and Qizil Uzun Rivers join to form the Sefid Rud, this 348-ft.-high, buttressed concrete dam was begun in 1956 and inaugurated by the Shah, accompanied by the Empress Farah, after whom it is named, in May 1962. It was built on behalf of the Plan Organization by French consultants and contractors. Its electric generating capacity is 87,500 kw.

131–132 TEHRAN OIL REFINERY

The steady increase in the internal consumption of pertroleum products and the need to reserve as much as possible of the Abadan refinery's output for export called for the construction of a centrally-located modern refinery to serve Persia's home needs. Hence the decision by the National Iranian Oil Company to build a refinery at Shahr-e-Rey, 9 miles south-west of Tehran.

The refinery was built for the N.I.O.C. by German and American consultants and contractors and was officially opened by the Shah in May 1968. It has a capacity of 80,000 barrels a day and produces motor gasoline, kerosene fuel and gas oil for sale within Persia. Its crude oil is brought 470 miles by pipeline from Ahwaz in Khuzistan province.

There are some sixty large storage tanks at Rey, for the various petroleum products refined there. As a precaution against fire they are spread over a wide area and are inspected daily by a man who does his rounds on a bicycle.

133 ABADAN REFINERY, CATALYTIC CRACKING PLANT AND STORAGE TANKS
In May 1901 an Englishman, William Knox d'Arcy, obtained a concession to prospect for oil in all but the northern provinces of Persia. Not until May 1908 was oil struck in commercial quantities at Masjid-e-Suleiman, in the southern foothills of the Zagros Mountains. A year later the Anglo-Persian Oil Company (now The British Petroleum Company Ltd) was formed in London to exploit this discovery. A pipeline was laid from the oil field to Abadan, a small island 130 miles away in the Shatt-al-Arab at the head of the Persian Gulf, where a refinery was completed in 1912. Such were the modest beginnings of today's mighty oil industry. As new oil fields were discovered, so the capacity of the refinery was increased from an initial $\frac{1}{4}$ million long tons per annum to 3 million tons in 1926 and 21 million tons in 1968.

The catalytic cracking plant breaks down waxy distillates, which would otherwise go into fuel oil, into much lighter components, used in high-grade products such as motor gasoline and liquefied petroleum gas.

134 KHARG ISLAND, PERSIAN GULF, LOADING JETTIES AND FEEDER LINES
The three-year-long Anglo-Persian oil dispute was finally settled with the ratification by the Majlis in October 1954 of an agreement between the Persian government and a Consortium of eight major oil companies, British, American, Dutch and French, known as the Iranian Oil Operating Companies. The rapid increase in oil exports which followed this agreement and the increasing use of large tankers called for an early expansion of port facilities. Hence the development between 1958 and 1966 of Kharg Island – a small neglected coral island 25 miles off the Persian mainland, directly on the deepest water line of the normally shallow Persian Gulf – into one of the great oil terminals of the world.

To achieve this, submarine pipelines were laid to bring the crude oil from the mainland, a task demanding engineering skill of the highest order. Initially, between 1958 and 1960, only crude oil from the rich Gachsaran field was exported from the island, but in 1964 it was decided to pump crude oil from all the Consortium's mainland oil fields to Kharg Island for loading. This required a major expansion and renovation of existing facilities, including increasing the number of 30-in. submarine pipelines from two to four and the number of tanker berths from four to ten, at an additional cost of about £33 million.

The jetty is now the world's largest and handles the biggest super-tankers afloat, which can be loaded at the phenomenal rate of over 10,000 tons per hour.

135–139 TRANS-IRANIAN GAS PIPELINE

The construction of one of the world's largest-diameter pipelines – 680 miles of 40-in. and 42-in. steel pipe – from Agha Jari in southern Persia to Astara on the south-west shore of the Caspian, where the frontiers of Persia and the USSR meet, is one of the most imaginative and epic achievements of modern Persia. For years, in the absence of economic transportation and marketing techniques, most of the natural gas associated with the production of crude oil from the southern Persian oil fields has been flared off and wasted. It was not until the Shah's State visit to the USSR in 1965 that broad agreement was reached whereby this valuable natural resource was to be piped and sold to the Soviet Union. In return for an eventual 1,050 million standard cubic feet per day to be delivered for fifteen years starting in 1970, the Russians undertook to provide Persia with a large long-term, low-interest credit to finance the building of Persia's first steel mill near Isfahan, and other projects including that section of the pipeline to be built by the Soviets.

The line crosses some of the most difficult and inaccessible terrain in Persia – from a starting-point 50 ft. above sea level it climbs to 9,500 ft. to cross the Zagros Mountains before descending to 50 ft. below sea level at its termination at Astara. Branch lines to Isfahan, Qum, Kashan, Shiraz and Tehran will provide gas for these towns and surrounding villages.

American, British, French and German, as well as Iranian and Russian engineers and contractors, were involved, while the consultants to the National Iranian Oil Company for the entire project were a British firm, the International Management and Engineering Group. The scenes shown here were taken deep in the Zagros Mountains over 100 miles south of Isfahan.

Each of these sections consists of two lengths of 42-in. pipe which have previously been 'double-jointed' by an automatic welding machine. Each section is 74 ft. long and weighs approximately 8 tons. They are strung out by the side of the ditch into which they will eventually be buried. First, however, the sections must be welded together and wrapped with an anti-corrosive plastic. A major logistical problem was that of transporting these sections of pipe from the Persian Gulf port to the points where they were needed, often in very rugged and hitherto inaccessible areas, requiring the construction of roads before they could be hauled in. Pipe for the project was supplied from Britain, France, Germany and Japan, as well as from an American-built pipe mill at Ahwaz, opened by the Shah in December 1967.

Frequently, a section of the pipe had to be cold-bent before it was welded into the line. For this purpose, a 150 h.p. American machine, which could cold-bend the pipe to any angle required, was used. This machine weighs 60 tons and utilizes hydraulic pressures of 2,500 lb. per square inch to bend the pipe, in which a mandrel is inserted to ensure that the circular cross-section is retained during the bending operation.

137 WELDING THE PIPE

Skilled Persians, working in pairs, welded the 42-in. pipe at a remarkable speed, taking about two hours to deposit 20 lb. of special high-tensile welding electrode. Each weld was scientifically inspected for possible faults prior to wrapping. In rugged terrain, up to 47 welds a day, covering over 1,100 yards, would be made; on flat ground the rate of progress would be trebled.

138 WRAPPING MACHINE

Another ingenious American machine, working at great speed and propelling itself forward as it worked, automatically removed rust and debris from the pipe, then applied and spread primer and finally wrapped the pipe with a double wrap of anti-corrosive plastic. This plastic was manufactured in the United Kingdom by one of the only two firms in the world specializing in the material.

139 LOWERING IN OF THE PIPE

The pipe, now welded and wrapped, is here being lowered into the ditch by two heavy Caterpillar tractors, fitted with side booms to lift and manoeuvre the pipe into position. On the steep slopes of the Zagros Mountains this was a particularly difficult operation requiring heavy tractors weighing 60 tons and equipped with 385 h.p. engines, provided with turbo-chargers to maintain horsepower in the thin mountain air. Once laid, the pipe is buried under earth.

140 MASJID-E-SULEIMAN, WELL ON FIRE

One of the hazards of drilling for oil or gas is that an escape of subterranean gas may be ignited by an unlucky spark before it can be brought under control. This is what happened in September 1968 at Masjid-e-Suleiman when drilling for gas to be used for the manufacture of petro-chemicals in the big new Irano-American plant at Bandar-e-Shapur at the head of the Persian Gulf; the fire raged for nearly two months before the combined efforts of experts from the United States, the United Kingdom and Persia were able to extinguish it. In the foreground, 400 yards from the flames, a relief well is being drilled. Mud and cement pumped into this well ultimately enabled the burning well to be controlled.

141 PRINCESS FARAHNAZ PAHLEVI (LATIYAN) DAM NEAR TEHRAN

Accompanied by the Empress and their two children, the Crown Prince and Princess Farahnaz (after whom the dam is named), the Shah formally opened this mass concrete, buttress-type dam at Latiyan on the Jaje River, 20 miles east of Tehran, in May 1967. The dam provides irrigation water for the Varamin plain south-east of Tehran, as well as much-needed drinking water for the capital, whose population has increased from 1.5 million in 1956 to over 2.7 million in 1966.

The well-known British firm, Sir Alexander Gibb & Partners, were the consulting engineers for this project, as they also are for a new dam which is planned to be built shortly across the Lar River in anticipation of an eventual doubling of Tehran's present population.

ACKNOWLEDGMENTS

I have attempted to include so comprehensive a selection of sites and monuments in this book, that it has been necessary for me to travel extensively within the vast area of modern Iran. To have done this within a reasonably short time would have been quite impossible had I not had the generous help and co-operation of many departments of the Government of Iran.

I have been honoured by being granted permission to take photographs in three holy shrines, those of Meshed, Qum and Rey. In the case of Meshed I am deeply conscious of the privilege conferred upon me, of being the first foreigner for very many years to work within the precincts of the Shrine of Imam Reza.

Primarily, however, I have to thank the Imperial Iranian Ministry of Foreign Affairs, and especially H.E. the Foreign Minister, Mr Ardeshir Zahedi, and through him, H.E. the Minister of Information, Mr Javad Mansur, and his Ministry for their generous hospitality, arrangements made for me, and provision of transport, especially to many remote areas, which alone made completion of this book a possibility.

Similarly, the help of the Department of the Prime Minister's office, the Iranian National Tourist Organisation, known as I.N.T.O., and its Director, H.E. Dr Ghassem Reza'i, whose interpreter-guides enabled me to travel freely throughout Persia without any problems or delays.

The support and counsel of H.E. the Minister of Culture, Mr Mehrdad Pahlbod, was very helpful. I should have liked to have more space to indicate the influence of successive Persian cultures in countries outside modern Iran, other than our single picture of the Sassanian arch at Ctesiphon.

Apart from those mentioned above, I have to thank especially the following:

In the Ministry of Information, the Under Secretary, H.E. Mr Farhad Nikhoukar, whose department arranged two long journeys for me in 1968; also the Ministerial Adviser on Foreign Relations, Mr Hassan Shahbaz, who did so much in the early stages of this book.

In I.N.T.O.—the Director of Tourist Facilities Division, Dr Moinuddin Marja'i and the Director of Public Relations, Mr Babak Sassan, have done much to aid me. Many officials of I.N.T.O. assisted me in their own areas—too many to list individually, but from whom I must select: Mr Ibrahim Tahsili at Shiraz, Mr Abbas Bayat at Isfahan, and Mr Mehdi Jala'i at Meshed. My invaluable guide and companion, Mr Tourej Kanani, and the Director of Photography, Dr Assadollah Beyrouzan, have been good friends and advisers.

My particularly warm thanks must be expressed to the Governor General of Khorassan Province, and Keeper of the Shrine at Meshed, H.E. Mr Bagher Pirnia, for the unique facilities he provided for me there. But many other Governors and Government officials have provided me with assistance and facilities, when often I have arrived unexpectedly after a long journey. My appreciation for their immediate hospitality must especially be expressed to the Governors of Gorgan, Qazvin and Darab.

The Ministry of Foreign Affairs generously arranged for me the facility of a helicopter at Isfahan to photograph the city and the surrounding countryside, so as to produce special pictures for this book.

The National Iranian Oil Company assisted me in visiting the oil areas around Abadan, and the ancient sites in the vicinity; the Iranian Oil Operating Companies made it possible for me to visit their Kharg Island terminal; the engineering consultants I.M.E.G. kindly flew me to photograph impressive pipeline-laying operations in the mountains west of Isfahan; officials of the Caspian Fisheries helpfully assisted me in visiting Bandar Shah and their factory there.

On a personal level I am deeply indebted for invaluable assistance and encouragement from several kind friends, but especially H.E. Mr Abbas Aram, Iranian Ambassador in London, and H.E. Mr Abdul Hamzavi, now Iranian Ambassador in Bangkok; Mr and Mrs David Holden; Mr Mahmud Poozeshi; Mr Arthur Harris of the Iranian Oil Participants Ltd; Mr David Stronach of the British Institute of Persian Studies, Tehran; Dr Wolfram Kleiss of the German Archeological Institute, Tehran; and Mr Ali Shapourian, now Press Counsellor at the Iranian Embassy, London.

I would also like to acknowledge the skill and experience which Mrs Pauline Baines has contributed to the preparation of the book as its Art Editor.

Finally, to my friend and collaborator in this book, Sir Denis Wright, British Ambassador in Tehran—my gratitude for his wise advice, and, with Lady Wright, for their combined assistance and generosity.

To all of these, and to many more unlisted here, my sincere thanks now expressed are insufficient acknowledgment of the help and courtesy they have all invariably shown me.

ROGER WOOD

INDEX

Numbers in italics refer to the plates, roman numerals to colour plates

215